ALEX RYVCHIN

ZIONISM

THE CONCISE HISTORY

Published in 2019 by Connor Court Publishing Pty Ltd

Copyright © ALEX RYVCHIN

All rights reserved. No part of this book may be reproduced or transmitted in any form or by any means, electronic or mechanical, including photocopying, recording or by any information storage and retrieval system, without prior permission in writing from the publisher.

ISBN: 9781925826586

Connor Court Publishing Pty Ltd

PO Box 7257
Redland Bay QLD 4165
sales@connorcourt.com
www.connorcourtpublishing.com.au

Printed in Australia

Front Cover Design: Ian James

"For more than two centuries, many millions of Christians and Jews – and, for that matter, many who were neither – were proud to call themselves Zionists, supporters of Zionism, the modern name of the oldest national movement in the world: the Jews returning to their ancient homeland, Zion. To cite just one prominent example, Winston Churchill's greatest living biographer, Andrew Roberts, writes that "The sole hero of that benighted period of the thirties, Winston Churchill, was a Zionist."

If any national movement should have earned humanity's support, and even awe, it should have been that of the Jews. And it did. Indeed, for many non-Jews – especially, but not only, Christians – the return of the Jews to Israel after 2,000 years of forced displacement and unique persecution was the most tangible example of a biblical prophecy come true.

Nor did the creation of Israel displace any other state. The only sovereign countries to have ever existed in the land called Israel, and later called "Palestine" by its Roman conquerors, were Jewish: the first Jewish state, which was destroyed in 586 BCE, and the second Jewish state, destroyed in the year 70 CE.

Yet today, "Zionist" is widely viewed as a term of opprobrium.

The only way to combat this latest expression of Jew-hatred – and what else can one call isolating only one country in the world, the Jewish country, as the target of economic and even physical destruction? – is through education.

That is why Alex Ryvchin's modern, scholarly, eminently readable, and fair history of Zionism is so important."

Dennis Prager

"Alex Ryvchin has written a clear, readable chronicle of Zionism that skillfully places the case for Israel in its true historical context."

John Howard OM AC, Former Prime Minister of Australia

"A fast-paced and unflinching history from a master writer. Ryvchin brilliantly chronicles the unbreakable 3,000-year-old bond between the Jewish people and the land of Zion and tells the story powerfully and definitively. A wonderful contribution to Jewish history."

Senator Linda Frum

"The clarity of Ryvchin's storytelling captures the essence of Zionism and explains the Jewish desire to return home in a manner that will fascinate, educate and inspire."

Isaac Herzog, Chairman of the Jewish Agency

"This important book should be read by all Zionists who need intellectual and historical ammunition to fight against anti-Zionists and by all who question Zionism out of ignorance or misguided political correctness."

Alan Dershowitz

"A must-read for anyone wishing to understand a movement that has somehow become a dirty word. It not only expertly charts the history of Zionism, but demonstrates why its counter movement is steeped in antisemitism. This book is brilliant."

Caroline Marcus, Sky News

"A compelling and contextualized history of the ancient idea that became one of the most successful revolutions of modern times."

Steve Ganot, *Israel Hayom*

"In our time, someone like Alex Ryvchin shouldn't be possible. His is a narrative voice that is at once searingly truthful, self-critical, inflected with moments of unspeakable tenderness, bordering on poetry, and blessedly free of the acrimony that pollutes so many sites of public disagreement. Few other voices could have told the story of Zionism that he tells here: in part, an account of the egregious inhospitality that has greeted Jews throughout the world, an historical 'never-at-home-ness' that made their diabolical displacement in the Shoah possible; in part, a testimony of unfailing hopefulness and political genius, animated by Ryvchin's distinctive moral energy that never descends into cant or hagiographic naïveté."

Scott Stephens, ABC

"The global anti-Israel campaign would like to make 'Zionism' a swear word. Alex Ryvchin's clear and compelling narrative restores to the word its proper nobility. He tells the story of a popular social movement that secured the universal democratic right of the Jewish people to national self-determination; a political movement that secured a refuge state in a world of antisemitism run wild; and a cultural movement that secured the spiritual and linguistic rebirth of the Jewish people in the land of its birth, a chapter in human affairs that still has the capacity to astonish."

Professor Alan Johnson
editor of *Fathom:* for a deeper understanding of Israel and the region

"A comprehensive, accessible history of Zionism that stretches from the period of exile under the Romans to the creation of Israel. Alex Ryvchin has distilled a complex movement to its essentials to provide audiences with an understanding of how Zionism came to be and why it was essential."

Seth Frantzman, *Jerusalem Post*

"A magnificent book, chilling, inspiring, deeply engrossing. Ryvchin tells the story of Zionism with grandeur and eloquence. He shows us the magnitude of the Zionist project, the scale of the achievement and that the battle to secure the rights and freedoms of the Jewish people is never-ending."

Rowan Dean, *The Spectator*

"A clear and beautifully written history of the Jewish national liberation movement. Ryvchin's book is essential reading."

Josh Hammer, The Daily Wire

To Vicki
best of wives and best of women

ABOUT THE AUTHOR

Alex Ryvchin was born in Kiev, Ukraine. His family left the Soviet Union as refugees and refuseniks in 1987, and settled in Sydney, Australia where Alex attended Sydney Boys High School before studying law and politics at the University of New South Wales.

He spent time as a researcher and speechwriter for a member of the state legislature before working as a lawyer at two of the world's largest law firms, first in Sydney and then in London. He was awarded an Israel Research Fellowship in 2012 and worked as a research fellow and staff writer at a Jerusalem-based think-tank.

In 2013 he joined the Executive Council of Australian Jewry, Australia's premier representative and advocacy body for the Australian Jewish community, and was promoted to co-Chief Executive Officer in February 2018, becoming one of the youngest leaders in the Jewish diaspora. He is a member of the Jewish Diplomatic Corps.

He writes and speaks around the world on the Arab-Israeli conflict, foreign affairs, antisemitism and the Holocaust, and religion and identity, and is a regular commentator on TV and radio.

His first book is the internationally acclaimed, *The Anti-Israel Agenda – Inside the Political War on the Jewish State*, (Gefen Publishing House, 2017).

He lives in Sydney with his wife, Vicki and daughters, Lilah and Elly, and is expecting a third daughter.

alexryvchin.com

ACKNOWLEDGMENTS

This book is the culmination of much toil; long days and nights spent reading, researching, contemplating, scribbling notes, striding streets gesturing like a madman to stimulate new ideas and refine old ones. But telling the story of Zionism and Jewish liberation has been a joyous experience. There was not a moment that I doubted what I was doing or why it needed to be done.

I wish to convey my deep gratitude to those who made publication of this book possible. My publishers, Connor Court, led by Anthony Cappello, have done an excellent job with this book. I am deeply grateful to Professor Alan Dershowitz for honoring me by writing the foreword. Alan is perhaps the finest advocate the Jewish people have had in recent times, and his fearless, brilliant and tireless endeavors are what every leader and advocate should aspire to. I thank my co-Chief Executive Officer at the Executive Council of Australian Jewry, Peter Wertheim AM for doing an excellent job of fact-checking and suggesting edits that strengthened the text. He is the consummate professional Jewish leader and I have benefited from working alongside him these years in more ways than I can appreciate.

I thank Jillian Segal AO, who is the most generous, devoted and able community leader I have known. I thank Jillian and John

Roth for supporting this book. I thank Greg Rosshandler for his kind words of praise over the years and for generously supporting this book.

I thank the exceptional professionals, leaders and advocates who I have been honored to learn from and work with – foremost among them Robert Goot AM SC and Gerald Steinberg. I thank Lynda Ben-Menashe for her guidance at the beginning of my career.

I am grateful to my parents for their boundless love and pride in me, and for endowing me with the twin pillars of my character – devotion to family and a love of the Jewish people.

I am grateful to my brother, Eugene, of the most blessed and highest memory, for teaching me daily both in life and in death, for showing me the beauty and preciousness of life and the need to make some mark on the world in the short time we are given, and for giving me the strength to overcome whatever stands before me. Thank you also for giving me my wonderful niece, Ariella and nephew, Isaac.

I thank my friends for making me laugh.

I thank my daughters, Lilah and Elly for calling me "papa" (and "monkey"), for needing me, and for filling each waking day and each waking night with so much love and happiness that my sleep-deprived brain is forced to convert it into pure contentment and productive energy.

I thank my wife, Vicki, who has been with me through every success and failure, and will so remain. She encourages me in everything I do. She is my companion and partner in life. Her pride in me drives me daily. She has gifted me two daughters and with another on the way. I deeply cherish her love and friendship.

ACKNOWLEDGEMENTS

This book is dedicated to her.

In determining that such a book needed to be written, I was conscious that the story of the Jews, the meaning of Zionism and the history of Israel was no longer being told by people like Martin Gilbert, Paul Johnson and Simon Schama, historians compelled by good faith and intellectual rigor. Instead, defining what it means to be a Zionist has been left to activists and political climbers whose starting point is an instinctive contempt for the very subject on which they write and opine. Consequently, millions of people have heard that Zionists supposedly collaborated with the Nazis or that Zionism is incompatible with feminism, long before they have learned what Zionism is or listened to the very people who identify with the cause of Jewish liberation. Allowing Zionism to be defined by anti-Zionists would be an injustice akin to allowing Klansmen to define the Civil Rights Movement.

Furthermore, while wonderful histories of the Jews and of the creation of the modern State of Israel have been written, a narrative history of Zionism, to be used by both Jews and non-Jews, students of history and the reading public, has not. Zionism, of course, straddles both Jewish and modern Israeli history, but it is a story of its own, an extraordinary one at that, and deserves a dedicated telling.

I hope that each reader will gain an understanding of what Zionism is, what it is not, and will take inspiration from the capacity of mortal men and women to transform a bold idea into the living embodiment of the redemption, the rescue, and the return of an ancient people.

CONTENTS

Acknowledgements	7
Foreword by Professor Alan M. Dershowitz	13
1 Zion	17
2 Thunder	31
3 J'Accuse!	45
4 London	55
5 Chemistry	65
6 Balfour's Note	79
7 Clash	105
8 Inferno	125
9 Israel	159
10 Anti-Zionism	195
Notes	217
Appendix	233
Index	239

FOREWORD
PROFESSOR ALAN M. DERSHOWITZ

Zionism is the national liberation movement of the Jewish people. It is one of the great human rights movements of the 20th century. The establishment of Israel as the nation-state of the Jewish people half a century after the first Zionist gathering in Basel in 1897 fulfilled the prophecy of its organizer Theodor Herzl, who just a year earlier had published his monumental pamphlet, The Jewish State. Herzl predicted in 1897 that within 50 years, a Jewish State would become a reality. He was off by a year.

Herzl, a secular Jewish playwright and journalist, had reported on the notorious trial of Alfred Dreyfus, the Jewish officer in the French army who was the victim of an antisemitic frame-up. Observing the pervasive Jew-hatred among the military, the church and much of the populace, Herzl concluded there was no future for Jews in Europe. His answer to the long-standing "Jewish question" was the establishment of a Jewish nation state in Eretz Yisrael— the biblical and post-biblical home of the Jewish people from which most Jews had been expelled. Some had remained and had lived in what came to be called Palestine for nearly two millennia. Indeed, even before Herzl wrote *The Jewish State*, Jews constituted a majority of the population of Jerusalem and a significant percentage of the population of other ancient cities.

Although Herzl did not quite predict the Holocaust and the murder of six million Jews, he did see the repeated pogroms, rampant discrimination and bigotry as the seeds of hatred that ultimately blossomed into the poisonous plants of genocide.

Israel was not built on the ashes of the Holocaust alone, as some have argued. By the time Winston Churchill visited Jewish Palestine in 1921, he already saw a flourishing pre-state with political parties, newspapers, hospitals, educational institutions and orchestras. Had the British not imposed racial and religious restrictions on entry to Palestine before and during the Holocaust, millions of Jews might well have been saved.

Following the establishment of the State of Israel, the nation-state of the Jewish people opened its doors to any Jew seeking asylum. Jews came to Israel from all over the world, fleeing oppression in Europe, North Africa, the Middle East and later the Soviet Union. These migrations into Israel were among the greatest human rights success stories in history.

Israel was born by the pen, though it had to be defended by the sword. Zionism was a theory, before it became a reality. Several Jewish writers, most prominently Leon Pinsker, anticipated Herzl's advocacy. Many more writers followed Herzl. Then there were declarations, treaties, and other written justifications for the establishment of Israel. The resolution in favor of a partition of Mandatory Palestine into two states for two peoples by the United Nations in 1947 was the culmination of many previous legal pronouncements.

It is not surprising that Israel has the most legitimate birth certificate of any modern democracy, because so many of its founders were legally trained. These include Herzl, Jabotinsky, Begin, and Shamir. What is more surprising was that this newly formed state was able to defend itself in war. Jews had not had an army for millennia, but when they were attacked by all the surrounding Arab states, as well as by Palestinian Arabs, they managed to cobble together a citizen army that defeated their enemies, who were determined to destroy Israel at its birth.

At the time of its establishment, Israel was one of the most popular countries in the world. It was beloved throughout Europe, perhaps out of guilt for what so many Europeans had done to Jews in the immediate past. Zionism was a word to which Jews and non-Jews pledged adherence. But following Israel's victory in the Six Day War in 1967, many on the hard left turned against Israel and Zionism, as the Soviet Union severed diplomatic relations and cast Zionists as criminals. The bigotry of the hard left has now spread to many young people on the center-left of politics who now see Zionism as a dirty word. Much of this change is based on ignorance and willful blindness. It has become politically incorrect to be a Zionist.

I am a proud Zionist and will always say so. In my book "Defending Israel: the story of my relationship with my most challenging client," I detail my 70-year history of Zionism and the reasons why it has been such an important part of my life for so many years.

That doesn't mean that I agree with every decision by every Israeli government. I am a proud American patriot, but that doesn't mean I agree with every decision made by my own country.

It is crucially important to distinguish Zionism -- which every reasonable person, regardless of party affiliation or ideology, should support — with particular Israeli policies or actions. Most Zionists who live in Israel understand this distinction, but too many American and European academics, students and left wingers do not. Israel is the only country in the world about which critics say: "I don't agree with Israel's position on West Bank settlements, therefore Israel has no right to exist."

This important book, *Zionism: the concise history*, makes a strong case for Zionism and a strong case against the bigotry of anti-Zionism. It should be read by all Zionists who need intellectual and historical ammunition to fight against anti-Zionists. It should also be read by all who question Zionism out of ignorance or misguided political correctness. They too, may learn why they are wrong.

-- Professor Alan M. Dershowitz

1

ZION

ZIONISM DEFINED

In its truest, simplest sense, Zionism refers to the return of the Jewish people to "Zion". The location of Zion has been variously interpreted as everything from a specific hill in Jerusalem known as Mount Zion, to the city of Jerusalem itself, and the entirety of the lands in which the Jewish people dwelled in biblical times. Throughout the history of the Jews, this notion of a return to Zion wavered between the rational and the mystical, manifesting in messianic visions of a kingdom restored and a world to come, humble migrations by families and communities, and grand projects for statehood and the mass ingathering of the exiles.

Zionism, as we understand it today, is neither a vague longing nor a mystical apparition. It is a precise political concept derived from a belief in or support for the right of the Jewish people to exercise national self-determination in some part of their ancient homeland. Launched as a political movement in the late 19th century, Zionism's purpose was to ingather some of the Jews, who were scattered throughout the world, into a single, national polity through which they could freely determine their political status and protect and enlarge those things that make the Jewish people distinct – their culture, languages, religion and heritage.

Zionism is also frequently referred to as a "national liberation movement", given its distinct aim of freeing the Jews from hatred, inequality and statelessness, while liberating the land from the grip of foreign empires that repeatedly fell upon it.

Before we examine how the idea of a Jewish national return to Zion was conceived, shaped and implemented, we need to first understand this attachment to Zion. What was it about that place that merited that nearly two millennia after their expulsion from it, the Jews would still be fighting to return?

ZION

The existence of a people and a society known as "Israel" can be traced more than 3,200 years to the dawn of the Iron Age. The oldest reference to a people called "Israel" located in roughly the territory of the modern State of Israel is to be found on a stone monument of the Egyptian Pharaoh Merenptah, son of Rameses II. This monument, which still stands in the Egyptian Museum in Cairo, records Merenptah's successful military campaigns in the Middle East and North Africa, notably against Libya, and refers also to battles in Ashkelon, Gezer and Yanoam in ancient Canaan. There it is proclaimed: "Israel is laid waste, his seed is not."[1]

Historians have noted that as early as the 13th century BCE, "Israel" referred to a socio-ethnic entity which consisted of a sedentary, agricultural society, significant enough to warrant mention in the Pharaoh's list of conquests.[2]

Much like its modern counterpart, early Israel rarely existed in tranquil anonymity. It was marked by internal ruptures and foreign conquest, the former often weakening it while the latter could serve to galvanize it into a force far greater than its meagre population or territorial possessions.

According to the Biblical account, the first Israelite king was Saul, who had been anointed by the Prophet Samuel in the belief that the middling warrior-leader would satisfy the people's demands to be ruled by a monarch rather than a prophet, while keeping real power in the hands of the prophet who had installed him. Saul's capacities were greater than Samuel had expected, and under his rule, the united Kingdom of Israel was established and began to flourish.

Saul's successor, King David, would prove to be Israel's finest king, as famous for his divine poetry as for his battlefield achievements. He remains the archetype to which many a Jewish leader still aspires.

The earliest archeological evidence of David's dynasty was recorded on a stone slab discovered in northern Israel in 1993 and dates back to the mid-eighth century BCE. The inscription tells of an Aramean king vanquishing several thousand Israelite and Judean horsemen and charioteers belonging to the "king of Israel" and the "House of David".[3]

When David ascended to the throne he took control of a united kingdom that was nevertheless still affected by tribal divisions. David's greatest achievement was in cementing national unity, which he duly consummated by the conquest of the prized Jebusite city of Jerusalem, a strategic gem perched on the high-ground outside the territory apportioned to any of the 12 Israelite tribes.

Under David, the city was enlarged and served as the capital of the unified Israelite state. David established state institutions, undertook town planning, administered taxation, expanded trade routes with neighboring lands and established glorious citadels and monumental buildings.[4]

In his final years, David meticulously planned what was to be his greatest feat yet, an architectural and national wonder that would elevate the status of Jerusalem to an even higher plane – a Temple dedicated to the God of Israel. But David did not live a long life and it was left to his son, Solomon, to expand Jerusalem as the royal city, to enhance the nation's modes of taxation and trade, and finally fulfil his father's vision by building the first Temple, also known as the Temple of Solomon, atop Mount Moriah.

What is known of the precise appearance of the Temple has been gleaned from various biblical and literary sources. Physical evidence of Solomon's Temple was destroyed as a result of subsequent historical events, including the razing of the temple in ancient times and the erection of two Islamic structures on the site, the Dome of the Rock and the al-Aqsa Mosque, which were built on the site in the 7th and 8th centuries CE respectively, and stand to this day. The Islamic authorities that currently administer the sites have steadfastly refused permission for any kind of archaeological investigation of the area.

We are told that Solomon's Temple was framed by two 40 foot high bronze pillars, a golden altar, cedar-lined floors and walls, and a screen of hanging gold beyond which was found the Holy of Holies, the most sacred religious and historical relics of the Jewish people such as the Ark of the Covenant and the staff of Moses.[5]

With the completion of the Temple, the Kingdom of Israel had a political and religious capital in Jerusalem, and a national and religious monument that would come to symbolize every phase of Jewish history from death and destruction to resilience and restoration. And the Israelites had achieved this more than a thousand years before the start of the Common Era.

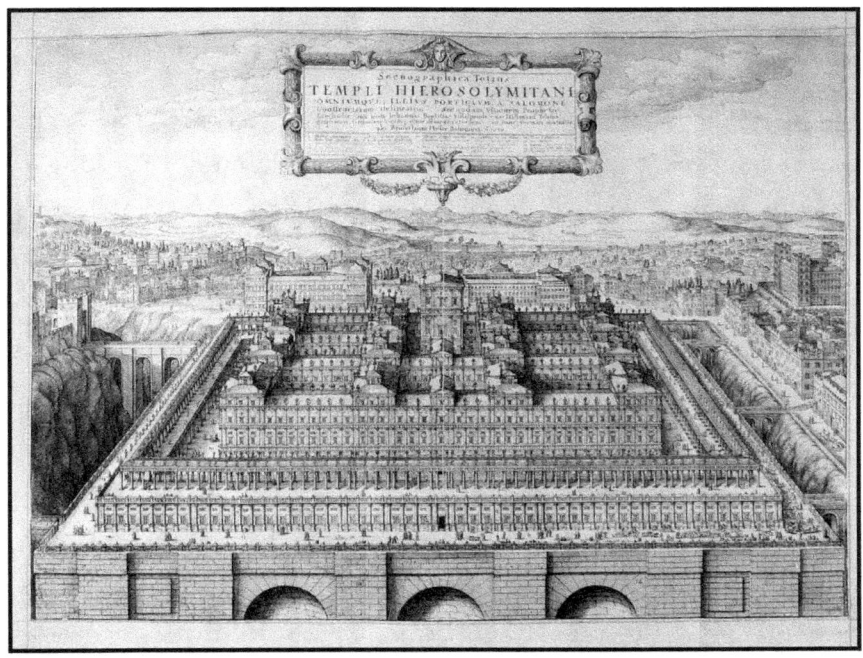

Engraving of Solomon's Temple from 1660 King James Bible (John Field, PBA).

BABYLON

Saul, David and Solomon had unified the people through a combination of brute force and diplomatic deftness. Upon the death of Solomon, the tribal passions and clannish feuds that had simmered below the surface split the kingdom into two, the northern kingdom of Israel and the smaller, southern kingdom of Judah. Divided, small in numbers, surrounded by mercantile and military powers in an age of expansion and conquest, the kingdoms had little prospect of surviving.

In 722 BCE, the northern kingdom of Israel was conquered and destroyed entirely by Assyria. Some of its inhabitants were carried off into a diaspora from which they would never return, assimilating completely with the peoples of the region, losing their distinct religious and national identity and becoming the near-mythical "lost tribes of Israel". Others are believed to have fled south and joined their Jewish brethren in Judah.

The southern kingdom of Judah survived, but not for long. In 587 BCE, on a day still mourned annually by observant Jews as "Tisha B'Av" (the 9th day in the Hebrew calendar month of Av), the forces of Babylon penetrated the walls of Jerusalem and razed Solomon's Temple. According to the ancient historian Josephus, the Temple had stood for 470 years.[6]

The Kingdom of Israel and its people had become a lost relic of history, and the Kingdom of Judah stood hopelessly defeated. To complete the subjugation of its people, the Babylonians carried 10,000 Jewish nobles, artisans and young men into exile in Babylon, leaving behind a population of mainly poor and aged who would be unable to mount an insurgency.

By the standards of those times, when tribes and clans emerged and disappeared, were routinely absorbed into greater civilizations or destroyed to a man, the Jews as a people stood on the precipice of vanishing entirely.

On this occasion, the Jews were saved from a long separation from their homeland. What began with a brutal conquest and forcible deportation ended with the fall of Babylon to Cyrus, the

Persian king. Cyrus duly permitted the Jews to return home to rebuild their holy temple in Jerusalem. Such were the whims and fancies of empires and rulers which would shape the destiny of the Jewish people for the next 2,000 years.

Though the Babylonian Exile lasted for a mere half century, it had a profound and permanent effect on the Jews as a people. It was in Babylon that the Jews had to grapple with being a people of the diaspora, living not in their own land but as foreign subjects in the lands of others. The Jews soon discovered that this was a dangerous and precarious form of existence.

Babylon also made the Jews more diligent in their religious observance and cultural practices, something that is frequently taken for granted when living as a majority within one's own country. Circumcision, observance of the Sabbath and high holidays all rigorously entered the Jewish liturgy and life-cycle.[7] Physically estranged from their land and denied the ability to exercise national self-determination, the Jews fell back on their customs and beliefs to impart order and rhythm to their new lives among the nations.

In Babylon, the Jews also developed a civic code that helped them to navigate the perilous terrain between living as exiles waiting to return, and assimilating fully into their surrounds, thereby discarding their unique laws, beliefs, languages and customs, and ceasing to be a distinct people like their lost Israelite brethren.

To guide them through their hardship, the Prophet Jeremiah wrote from Jerusalem to the Jewish leaders in Babylon, counselling them to "seek the welfare of the city where I have sent you into exile, and pray to the Lord on its behalf, for in its welfare you will find your welfare".[8] Jeremiah's decree was, and remains, the essence of good citizenry.

Jeremiah went further in his instructions. He urged the Jewish community in Babylon "to multiply there, not decrease", and to "build houses and settle down… and to plant gardens and eat their produce."[9] In other words, the Jews were to accept their new reality and make the most of it. They were to integrate fully and see themselves as a part of their new society.

But the Jews were never to accept their condition as one of permanence, nor were they to forget where they came from and to where they must strive to return.

Jeremiah reminded the Jews that their homeland still awaited them, declaring that the Jews would be "brought back from captivity … and will be gathered from all the nations and places."[10]

GREECE

Just as the rise of Persia saw the demise of Babylon, the rise of Greece transferred regional influence to Europe and saw the decline of Persia as an imperial power. The young Hellenic king, Alexander passed through Judea and was generally well disposed to its people, who in tribute took to naming their sons in honor of the Macedonian conqueror.

But at the end of Alexander's short life, his empire fractured under the weight of rival claimants to its spoils. The Jewish kingdom became a province of the Seleucid dynasty of Greece which ruled in Syria. Soon the Jews would be ruled by a tyrant, one Antiochus Epiphanes, who was intent on squeezing his dominions for all their worth and imposing Hellenic culture by grotesque and brutal means. Jewish rituals like circumcision and the observance of the Sabbath, holy rites that had sustained the Jews through their exile in Babylon, were outlawed, as was possessing copies of the Torah, the Jewish scriptures comprised of the Five Books of Moses. Altars for the offering of pigs flesh, a profanity to the Jews, were installed in the Temple in Jerusalem. When the persecution and desecrations became too much to bear, the Jews retreated to the Judean hills and waged a determined guerilla war that led to the liberation of Jerusalem, the expulsion of the Seleucid tyrant and the purification of the Jewish Temple in what is still commemorated as the Festival of Lights, Chanukah.

The defeat of the Greeks was impressive as a military campaign. More than that, it demonstrated the strength of the human desire to live free, and what the Jews were willing to do and willing to risk to hold onto their rights and freedoms.

ROME

The next stanza of the story of Zion saw the Jews pitted against the irresistible might of Rome. As we have seen, in the time of the early Jewish states, empires rose and fell and their contact with the Jews was often disastrous but also fleeting. The encounters with Egypt, Babylon, Assyria, Persia and Greece had nurtured a Jewish tradition that glorified resistance and internalized a belief in the Jews that no matter how formidable the foe, no foreign ruler could long suppress Jewish self-expression or keep them from living in their own land. But Rome was a different proposition. The Roman Empire at the beginning of the Common Era was not a fallen giant like the Greeks the Jews encountered or a transient regional power like Babylon centuries before. Rome was cutting edge, capable of waging long and devastating military campaigns on multiple fronts, and its presence was ubiquitous.

The culmination of all of this was a series of Jewish-Roman wars, which ended in slaughter, grief, dislocation and chaos on a scale the Jews would not experience again until the Holocaust.

Roman rule over Judea began after the conquest by Pompey in 63 BCE. By 66 CE, the suppression of Jewish national and religious rights again led to revolt. But on this occasion, the Jewish population was highly factionalized and much of the early fighting took the form of bloody skirmishes between rival sects. Josephus observed that there was "perpetual slaughter" as grim knife-wielding bandits fought the foot-soldiers of petty warlords.[11] It was Jew against Jew.

When the fighting eventually matured into a revolt against Roman rule, Rome's new emperor, Vespasian deployed his son, Titus to crush the Jewish resistance. Supported by 60,000 seasoned and well-equipped men, Titus's forces employed tactics of siege to break the Jewish resistance, finally slaughtering the Jews who were mad with hunger, taking more slaves than they knew what to do with, and hauling away the surviving captured to die in colosseums throughout the empire for the amusement of their subjects.

Josephus recorded in gruesome detail the culmination of the failed uprising, the destruction of the Second Temple:

> While the sanctuary was burning, looting went on right and left and all who were caught were put to the sword. There was no pity for age, no regard for rank; little children and old men, laymen and priests alike were butchered; every class was held in the iron embrace of war, whether they defended themselves or cried for mercy ... And how many who were wasted with hunger

and beyond speech, when they saw the Sanctuary in flames, found strength to moan and wail.[12]

The Destruction of the Temple of Jerusalem, depicted by Francesco Hayez.

With the Temple burnt to the ground and the resistance smashed, the last of the Jewish fighters decamped to various outposts, the final and most dramatic being the glorious Masada, a 1,300 foot high fortress in the Judean desert. There, the last of the rebels committed mass suicide, leaving behind well-stocked storerooms to show that their act was motivated by the pride of rebellion and not by desperation or hunger.

Some 60 years later, in 132 CE, under the leadership of Simon Bar Kokhba, the Jews again attempted to throw off Roman rule. They encountered the exceptionally cruel Roman emperor Hadrian who brutally suppressed the revolt by 135 CE. Hadrian despised eastern religions and was determined to crush Jewish particularism and connection to the land once and for all. To this end, he renamed Jerusalem, "Aelia Capitolina", erected a pagan temple on the site of the two Jewish temples, and forbade Jews from even entering the city on pain of death. Judea now became a province of Greater Syria, and was renamed, Syria-Palaestina. The latter name was associated with the extinct Philistines, who had for a time occupied the coastal lands and plains, mainly around today's Gaza and Ashkelon, but who had ceased to exist as a discernible people in 600 BCE.

The ruin of the Jews was near-complete. Zion was gone both in name and in fact. The Jewish remnants were mostly scattered throughout the Roman Empire where they would remain for two millennia through Inquisitions and infernos.

But several incidents indicated that Hadrian's determination to erase the Jews as a distinct people by severing their association with their land, was destined to fail.

One outer wall of the Second Temple complex built by the returned exiles from Babylon and enlarged by King Herod, remained standing. Jerome, writing his Commentary on Zephaniah some three centuries after the time of Hadrian, observed the following spectacle:

> On the day of the destruction of Jerusalem, you see a sad people coming to visit, decrepit little women and old men encumbered with rags and years ... they weep over the ruins of the Temple.[13]

Josephus tells us that prior to ordering the Temple burned to the ground, Titus convened his council of war to determine what was to be done with it. Some insisted that the entire structure should be turned into a smoldering heap or else it will "remain a rallying point for Jews all over the world" and would lead to "continual revolts".[14]

A story often told on the day of Tisha B'Av, which commemorates the destruction of both the first and second temples, recalls Napoleon walking by a Paris synagogue on this day, hearing the lamentations and loud weeping of the Jews. In the story, he asks one of his retinue what the Jews were crying about, and after being told about the destruction of the Temple nearly two millennia before, Napoleon remarked: "A nation that cries for 2,000 years for their land and Temple will return one day to their land to see it rebuilt."[15]

The Roman generals believed that so long as any structure stood in Zion, it would rally Jews worldwide to it. Jerome's account of the scene there on the festival of Tisha B'Av is testament to that. But the generals failed to appreciate the basis of the connection between people and land. As with all peoples dispossessed of their indigenous lands, where the ability to live on the land itself is lost, the connection to land is maintained by integrating it into the culture, ritual and storytelling of the people, generation to generation.

In this way, Jerusalem and the entirety of the lands of the Jewish states became exalted. They were remembered daily by Jews who would turn in prayer towards the holy city of Jerusalem. The memory of successful rebellion and the prize of national sovereignty was recalled on the Chanukah festival. The tragedy of the loss of lands and the destruction of the temples was mourned on Tisha B'Av. The central prayer of Jewish liturgy, the *Amidah*, which is recited thrice daily by observant Jews, would direct "the remembrance of Jerusalem", and mentions the holy city three times in total. "Zion" is mentioned three times as well. The annual Passover *Seder*, the most observed of Jewish rituals, concludes with the words, "Next year in Jerusalem", to signify that the full completion of the escape from bondage can only be achieved through a return to Zion.

From a military point of view, Hadrian and Titus's generals had achieved a total conquest of the Jews. Jewish statehood was gone, their precious Temple smoldered, the remaining pockets of stubborn armed resistance had been brutally broken. All that remained were small communities mainly in the Galilee region, in towns like Tsfat and Tiberias, also in Hebron, and following the death of Hadrian and the eventual lapsing of laws prohibiting Jewish entry into Jerusalem, the Jews gradually returned and settled there also.

But Hadrian's ultimate plan to obliterate the Jewishness of Jerusalem and the surrounding lands had failed. Jewish life in the land, while depleted, carried on. While for the Jews now living in exile, Zion shifted from their hands, no longer something to be possessed and touched, and came instead to animate their dreams and visions, and to inhabit their entire worldly consciousness.

2

THUNDER

From the time the Jews were first exiled from their homeland by the Babylonians, more Jews would live outside the territory of a Jewish state than within it. In 2018 CE, 43% of the world's Jews lived in Israel, constituting the highest percentage of the total world Jewish population living in their native lands for at least 2,000 years.

From the time the Jews were expelled from their homeland by Roman emperors in the first two centuries of the Common Era, the Jews had grown accustomed to being a people of the diaspora. Indeed, as we have seen, the process of acclimating to strange new surrounds and daunting realities spawned a rich stream of jurisprudence which sought to strike a balance between being a good, well-integrated citizen while still remaining a good and faithful Jew.

But the Jews would soon find that no matter how adaptive they were, no matter how loyal or lawful their ways, nothing could shield them from the harsh realities of living as a peculiar minority in the nations of others.

The history of the Jews in the diaspora from the second

Roman expulsion in 135 CE to the reestablishment of a sovereign Jewish state in 1948 CE, is a cornucopia of toil and hardship, prosperity and destitution, movement and upheaval, rejection and acceptance, hope and false dawns, and death and destruction on a scale that causes the travails under Rome to pale into near insignificance.

For the most part, the Jews were swept up in movements and continental trends far greater than them. Periods of puritanism in Europe and the Islamic world invariably saw the Jews persecuted, exploited, discarded and often butchered. But with human progress and enlightenment came expanded rights, periods of calm and prosperity, and even legal equality.

Times of darkness were usually darkest for the Jews who had come to live as secluded, easily identifiable and idiosyncratic elements of foreign societies. In Fez, Morocco in the year 1033, a Muslim tribe killed over 6,000 Jewish subjects, looting their possessions and committing atrocities against the Jewish women. In Spain and Portugal, Jews were forcibly converted on pain of death or expelled. In Lisbon in 1506 they were burned alive in public squares. In York in 1190, the entire Jewish community was set upon and murdered or forced into mass suicide. Wealth, status, age, sex or infirmity never saved the Jews from mob violence.

But the Enlightenment brought respite and opportunities for the Jews. In Hungary, Joseph II issued a decree shortly after ascending to the throne that immediately annulled the plethora of anti-Jewish laws that had confined the Jews to an institutionally inferior status. In France, the decline of the Church and the age of revolution brought with it a public examination of how the Jews should be treated in a new France.

In 1789, the French National Assembly debated whether Jews would be eligible for citizenship. One of the speakers, the Count of Clermont-Tonnerre expressed the position as follows: "The Jews should be denied everything as a nation, but granted everything as individuals."[1]

Another speaker, the Bishop of Clancy queried whether the Jewish attachment to Zion was compatible with integration into a modern France: "must one admit into the family a tribe that constantly turns its eyes toward another homeland?"[2]

After the debate fell in favor of granting equality, the Jews enthusiastically applied for citizenship and were finally emancipated and given full legal rights as individual citizens in France in 1791.

These dual experiences of wanton persecution and slow liberation gave rise to two distinct movements in the Jewish diaspora. When seeking to answer the question of how to secure for the Jews an existence of calm and equality, some would point to the French experience that with loyalty, participation and industriousness they would demonstrate their value to the nation and in turn be granted rights equal to those of non-Jewish citizens.

Others would carry with them the long memory of Jewish history to argue that emancipation was an illusion and that the conception of the Jew as the "other" was so deep, immutable and convenient that without a national centre the Jews living in foreign lands would merely limp from one calamity to the next.

In Eastern Europe, the dichotomy was most profound. Having continually migrated to escape oppression in England, France and Spain in the Middle Ages, the Jews had established major communities in Poland and Russia. By 1897, the Russian Empire was home to more Jews than any other part of the world.

The spirit of the Enlightenment that was liberating the Jews of Western Europe and spawned hope for universal acceptance, was slow in moving eastward. Still, many Russian Jews believed that even in their haphazard existence with Tsars and serfs, civil wars and changing borders, and a bounty of laws keeping Jews in a permanent state of wretched subordinacy, equality could still be won.

But amidst the hope and despair, the gains and setbacks, there was one factor that would foremost determine the destiny of the Jews of Russia and hovered over them at all times like a thunderous cloud ready to breach – *Pogrom*.

POGROM

The word "pogrom" literally means a strike of thunder. It was the term given to the frenzied mob violence that was inflicted on Jews by their neighbors throughout the diaspora. The intensity of pogroms varied. Some of these attacks achieved the complete annihilation of Jewish communities. Sometimes they were spontaneous or sparked by a personal dispute between a Jew and their non-Jewish neighbor. Often they had nationalistic motives and came in times of war and political upheaval unconnected to the Jews. Some fell on Christian holy days when religious fervor peaked. Some were sanctioned by governments, even led by police units or army detachments, stoked by newspapers, influential nobles or government officials. In most cases, they caused utter devastation and were marked by cruelty and depravity. Rape, decapitation, slaughter of women and children were all routine.

While the term "pogrom" is a Russian one, and indeed the practice was perfected on the soil of the Russian Empire, the concept of the pogrom accompanied the Jews throughout their wanderings.

In York in 1190, a devastating pogrom extinguished the Jewish community there entirely as noblemen looking to erase debts to Jewish creditors urged peasants into diabolical action. In Granada in 1066, a Muslim mob crucified a Jewish courtier and then murdered some 4,000 Jews spurred on, according to Bernard Lewis, by an antisemitic poem which in part read:

> Do not consider it a breach of faith to kill him, the breach of faith would be to let them carry on.[3]

In Germany in 1819, shortly after the emancipation of the Jews there, a series of riots known as "Hep-Hep", after the rallying cry used to summon the masses to violence against the Jews, resulted in widespread looting and murder in Frankfurt, Leipzig, Dresden, and Darmstadt.

These attacks became so commonplace and were carried out with such impunity that it soon took the barest pretense to justify their instigation. In France, the Bishop of Nancy in his testimony before the French National Assembly on the eligibility of Jews for citizenship, recalled interviewing Frenchmen intent on pillaging the homes of their Jewish neighbors. The justifications given to the Bishop included that "the Jews banded together too much" and had "bought the most beautiful homes."[4]

Portrait of Bogdan Chmelnitsky.

CARNAGE

The Cossack rebellion against Polish rule in the mid-17th century in what is now Ukraine, led by Bogdan Chmelnitsky resulted in the most devastating sequence of pogroms experienced before the Holocaust era. As the Cossacks rampaged through the country, the quest of political liberation quickly morphed into a bloodsport of murder and pillage levelled at hundreds of Jewish towns and villages. The very name "Chmelnitsky", whose statue still stands in Kiev, lives in infamy in Jewish history. The death toll from Chmelnitsky's barbarism stood in excess of one hundred thousand, with whole Jewish communities that had lived peaceably in the land for generations, disappearing entirely.

What remained was a deep gash in the collective Jewish psyche. It wasn't merely the scale of the massacres but the frightful abandonment of any human qualities by the attackers, that lived longest in the Jewish national memory. The fear of the demented, ribald cackle of the pogromist would never leave the Jews of Russia.

The historian Nathan Hannover recorded the following account of the butchery:

> Some of them had their skins flayed off them and their flesh was flung to the dogs. The hands and feet of others were cut off and they were flung unto the roadway where carts ran over them and they were trodden underfoot by horses. And some of them had many non-fatal wounds inflicted on them, and were flung out into the open so that they should not die swiftly but should suffer and bleed until they died. And many were buried alive. Children were slaughtered at their mothers' bosoms and many children were torn apart like fish. They ripped up the bellies of pregnant women, took out the unborn children, and flung them in their faces. They tore open the bellies of some of them and placed a living cat within the belly and left them alive thus, first cutting off their hands so that they should not be able to take the living cat out of the belly ... and there was never an unnatural death in the world that they did not inflict upon them.[5]

The incomprehensible sadism of the massacres called into question the very nature of the human race. For the Jews, it imparted a permanent dose of terror, nervous energy and insecurity that would be passed down like a hereditary trait. It also established a perverse instinct for ultra-violence among the perpetrators that could lie dormant for decades and then ferociously awaken with the collapse of societal order.

The question, asked centuries later, of how civilians in lands occupied by Nazi Germany could aid the invaders and turn on their Jewish neighbors with such enthusiasm, cruelty and zeal can largely be answered by reviewing the precedents set by Chmelnitsky's forces and the actions of regular folk that took part in the carnage and revelry. When a survivor of the Babi Yar massacre of Jews in Kiev during the Holocaust recorded that soldiers and Ukrainian auxiliaries were "laughing happily as if they were watching a circus act,"[6] as women and children were stripped naked and shot, the survivor could just as easily have been describing the crimes of Chmelnitsky's marauding horsemen committed in the very same land.

In *Down and Out in Paris and London,* a young George Orwell recalls a conversation with a retired Russian army officer who had contact with Jews during his service. "Have I ever told you, *Mon Ami,* that in the old Russian Army it was considered bad form to spit on a Jew? Yes, we thought a Russian officer's spittle was too precious to be wasted on Jews."[7] So inferior were the Jews of Russia considered that the Cossacks may well have reasoned they were mutilating livestock or delousing a contaminated field when they were destroying the lives of old communities composed of ordinary families.

Heightening the sense of abandonment and powerlessness of the Jews, after each bout of pogroms, the government at best did nothing, at worst it imposed even greater restrictions on the Jews.

After pogroms in Russia in 1881, the government introduced sweeping anti-Jewish legislation, known as the May Laws. The logic being that for the peace-loving native population to unleash such devastation on the Jews, the Jews must have acted in provocation and had to be restored to their rightful, inferior place, to keep passions in check. It was the same dark manipulation that was adopted by the Nazis in 1938 – inciting the devastating anti-Jewish pogrom known as *Kristallnacht,* and then using the violence as a pretext to escalate the persecution of the very people who had suffered.

When 19th century Russian conquests of territory in what is now Poland, Ukraine and the Baltic republics resulted in some five million Jews falling under the dominion of the Empire, the Russians now had a "Jewish problem" to be solved. The attitude to this problem of unwanted human stock was captured by the Russian Finance Minister Count Serge Witte in a conversation with Theodor Herzl:

> I used to say to the late Tsar, Alexander III, "Majesty, if it were possible to drown 6 or 7 million Jews in the Black Sea, I would be absolutely in favor of that. But if it is not possible, one must let them live.[8]

Graciously allowed to live, save for the periodic outburst of mob violence, the Jewish existence was governed by an extraordinary catalogue of laws that regulated every aspect of their lives. Where they could live, where they could study, where they could enter, work, travel, were all bound up by cruel, discriminatory laws that resulted in daily humiliations, exploitation, an existence of pure misery and a state of permanent anxiety in which even daily interactions seemed full of peril. Legislatively reduced to lesser people, the Russian Empire sent a message to its subjects that the Jews were people of no worth to be treated as mood or fancy should dictate.

The impact of all this on the history of Zionism cannot be overstated. It is no coincidence that the early writing about the formation of a political movement to achieve a mass return to Zion largely originated in the Russian Empire. Nor is it any wonder that the early migration to what Hadrian had renamed Palestine, ebbed and flowed with the anti-Jewish riots that took place in Eastern Europe.

The perpetual sense of lurking fear that was a consequence of the regular bouts of violence, inserted an urgency into the conversation about the future of the Jews. Could the Jews really feel at home in a country where rape, torture and pillage visited them in every generation, and when authorities entrusted to protect them, either stood complicit or stood idle? Was there a sincere path to equality and peace through citizenship as offered after the French Revolution or was this mere fantasy in a country where antisemitism had been elevated to a patriotic duty?

Leon Pinsker, author of the seminal work on *Zionism, Auto-Emancipation: An Appeal to His People by a Russian Jew* (Public Domain).

SELF-HELP

The phenomenon of the pogrom and the debased state in which Jews were forced to survive, triggered a series of awakenings among Jewish intellectuals and thinkers in search of a way out of the despair.

Leon Pinsker was one such notable. A student of the law and a practicing physician, Pinsker was a assimilated Russian Jew. He initially argued that the spread of liberalism would have a soothing effect on sectarian and religious tension and that by full immersion in Russian literary, cultural and scientific life, the Jew would gain equality.

Periodic outbreaks of unrest were not sufficient to shake his convictions but the violence of 1881 was too severe to ignore. Following the assassination of Tsar Alexander II, the strike of the pogrom hit Jews in nearly 200 villages and cities. What disturbed Pinsker the most was that the fuel for the attacks came not from the rage of the peasants but from the pens of the intellectuals. The writers and theorists which Pinsker revered and directed his people to aspire to had violently rejected any possibility of tolerance. The grim reality of the 1881 pogroms turned Pinsker from an ardent assimilationist into a Jewish nationalist. He penned the searing *Auto-Emancipation: An Appeal to His People by a Russian Jew*, the following year.

Pinsker spoke of the Jews lacking "geographic cohesion", which resulted in their being viewed with suspicion and contempt by the host nation. "Since the Jews are nowhere at home," he wrote, "nowhere regarded as a native, they remain aliens everywhere…" The result of this, Pinsker argued, was that the Jews were seen as a peculiarity, a relic, an ancient people who once possessed a homeland, now wandering the earth like "a ghost-like apparition of a living corpse." The Jew "lived everywhere but was never in their correct place."[9]

Pinsker's text had a scintillating effect. He had understood the nature of antisemitism as something both irrational and permanent and conceived a practical, implementable solution to the Jewish condition of despair. He wanted a return to Zion but the urgency of the moment briefly prevailed over any historical or religious attachment. "Perhaps the Holy Land will be ours again," he wrote but his priority was a place of "secure and undisputed refuge, capable of flourishing".

Pinsker's combination of the idealistic with the practical became a model for Zionist thinkers, ensuring that the idea of a return to national self-government was sufficiently romantic to capture the imagination and sufficiently grounded to hold the mind.

Pinsker died ten years after the pogroms of 1881 that shattered his naiveté and spawned the concept of self-liberation. His aspiration of convening a Jewish congress to organize the Jews into a coherent political force remained unfulfilled. But migration to Palestine did take place, more as an organic reaction to the injustices of 1881 than as part of an organized political program. The Jewish agricultural settlements in Palestine that Pinsker had envisaged were taking shape. Rishon LeZion, Rosh Pinna, Zikhron Yaakov, Hedera, all now major towns and cities in modern Israel, sprouted in the few years after the publication of Pinsker's work.

In the two decades that followed publication of *Auto-Emancipation,* some 40,000 Jews migrated to Palestine in what came to be known as the First Aliyah (meaning "ascent" in Hebrew).

Pinsker's calls for Jewish self-liberation and a return to statehood soon drifted into the coffee houses and the raucous communal debates of Western Europe. Within mere decades, Pinsker's vision would materialize.

3

J'ACCUSE!

DREYFUS

The trial of Captain Alfred Dreyfus is one of the most intriguing and significant episodes of the 19th century. Its plot would have been too grandiose for a compelling story of fiction. Yet the real life events surrounding the demise of a French officer captivated the nation, and had a monumental impact on modern history, and the path of the Jewish people. The Dreyfus Affair was to the father of modern Zionism, Theodor Herzl what the descending apple was to Isaac Newton and the laws of gravity.

On September 26, 1894, French Intelligence intercepted a message believed to be from an artillery officer on the general staff of the French Army. The message contained classified information that was being passed by the messenger to the German Military Attaché, Lieutenant-Colonel von Schwartzkoppen. Among the classified information passed to the Germans were details of new weaponry being developed by the French. The discovery two years later of further leaked communications matched the handwriting of the original intercepted message, and revealed the identity of the traitor to almost certainly be Ferdinand Walsin Esterhazy.

Esterhazy was an infantry major of dubious repute, frequently in debt, he once tried to swindle his own nephew using forged documents. He was eventually turfed out of the army on the charge of "habitual misconduct". Nevertheless, suspicion did not immediately fall on Esterhazy.

When the leak to the Germans was discovered, an investigation was duly conducted, which established that the culprit could only be one of half a dozen possible officers who had access to the classified information. One of the suspects was Captain Alfred Dreyfus, a career soldier with an unblemished record. Dreyfus had been motivated to serve in the military from a young age after seeing the loss and dislocation caused by the Franco-Prussian War in 1870. He was the only Jew on the general staff and quickly caught the attention of French intelligence and was arrested.

Colonel Sandherr, commander of the French military's counter-espionage service, promptly conveyed a message to the French Foreign Minister that the traitor had been apprehended: "The officer charged with treason is a Jew," Sandherr remarked, "... his false and conceited character, in which one recognizes all the pride and all the ignominy of his race, have made him suspect for a long time."[1]

Following his arrest, Dreyfus was tried, convicted and courtmartialed on the charge of high treason. In the courtyard of the École Militaire in Paris, a warrant-officer cut off the badges and buttons from Dreyfus's military dress, then removed the ceremonial sword from his scabbard and snapped it across his knee. All the while Dreyfus wretchedly professed his innocence and shouted, "long live France! Long live the Army!" Dreyfus was then deported and incarcerated in solitary confinement on the treacherous Devil's Island.

The trial of Dreyfus was conducted in closed session, but a leak from the military headquarters to the publisher of an antisemitic newspaper soon ensured the public was made aware that a Jewish officer stood accused of treason against the French Republic. As Dreyfus was paraded around the courtyard like a captured slave of Rome, a crowd of Frenchmen had gathered and chanted, "Death to Dreyfus!" and "Death to Jews!"[2]

The public degradation of Captain Alfred Dreyfus
(Henri Meyer, Public Domain).

HERZL

But Captain Alfred Dreyfus was not the star of this production. He was a mere bit player. Watching the public disgrace of Dreyfus was the 34-year-old Paris correspondent for the Viennese daily newspaper, *Neue Freie Presse,* Theodor Herzl. Herzl was a highly assimilated Austro-Hungarian Jew, meticulously groomed and known for his impeccable dress attire, and long dark beard and thick, slicked hair. He represented a picture of Jewish integration and European sophistication. He was a journalist, a playwright, and novelist of moderate acclaim and while devoid of religious practice and unspoken in Hebrew, he had a simmering interest in the Jewish question. A self-practicing assimilationist, he had also tinkered with the concept of Jewish nationhood as a cure to antisemitism.

The Dreyfus Affair transformed Herzl. It had the same effect on him that the 1881 pogroms had on Pinsker. In the public degradation of Dreyfus, Herzl had witnessed a matinee dramatization of the very theories and ideas with which he had been coming to terms. Herzl had once even considered conversion to Christianity as the antidote to antisemitism, so committed he was to the idea of Jewish assimilation. "They must disappear into the crowd", he wrote of the Jews of Europe.[3] But if a Jew like Dreyfus, loyal, civic, who had carved out a fine career in the French army, could be plucked from the very crowd where the Jews ought to have been safe, and then publicly humiliated and thrown into a secluded island prison for no crime, what safety could Herzl find for himself or for any Jew?

The pogroms had shown Pinsker that the advent of liberalism would not dislodge the ingrained hatred of Jews in Russia. Dreyfus showed Herzl that the emancipation of the Jews and citizenship and legal equality had done nothing to dampen suspicion and contempt for French Jews. All that was needed for a return to base instincts was a spark and an excuse. The antisemitic riots that spread through France following the literary defence of Dreyfus by the great French novelist, Emile Zola, underscored the point that the Jews, no matter how integrated and comfortable, were living in a fraying state of self-delusion.

Within six months of the Dreyfus trial, Herzl had hastily completed the first draft of his seminal work, *The Jewish State*. When the finished work was published it was printed in extract in the London paper, the *Jewish Chronicle* so that its ideas could begin to take effect on British Jewry, and from there, it was hoped it would begin to penetrate the highest echelons of British power.

Herzl was something of a rarity. He was prim and pompous, wildly ambitious, romantic and idealistic, and yet firmly rooted in practical affairs and endowed with a feverish appetite for hard work.

His manifesto combined the ideal of "the restoration of the Jewish State", with a precise plan for the lawful acquisition of land and the physical relocation of Jews from the diaspora to the new homeland. He wrote of the establishment of a Jewish Chartered Company domiciled in London to effect the disposal of Jewish assets, while the Society of Jews would secure land in the new country. Herzl had plans for a seven-hour working day, the migration of unskilled laborers from Russia and Romania to work the land, and plans for rudimentary manufacturing of clothing, linens and shoes.

Herzl, now burning with the injustice of the Dreyfus trial, began his treatise by articulating the problem:

> We have honestly endeavored everywhere to merge ourselves into

the social life of surrounding communities and to preserve the faith of our fathers. We are not permitted to do so. In vain are we loyal patriots, our loyalty in some paces running to extremes; in vain do we make the same sacrifices of life and property as our fellow-citizens; in vain do we strive to increase the fame of our native land in science and art, or her wealth by trade and commerce. In countries where we have lived for centuries we are still denounced as strangers."[4]

And then combined it with a stirring call to action:

The Jews who wish for a state will have it. We shall live at last as free people on our own soil, and die peacefully in our own homes.

These sentiments were then bound into a single, poetic epithet of hope and aspiration: "If you will it, it is no dream," which was contained in Herzl's utopian novel, *Altneuland* (Old New Land), published in 1902. The work gave further flesh and spirit to the ideas contained in *The Jewish State*.

After the Dreyfus Affair, Herzl's life was consumed with the mission of restoring the Jews to their homeland. He was an inexhaustible diplomat – writing, persuading, cajoling, travelling, seeking audiences, in order to win support for the idea both among the Jewish leadership and the Kaisers, sultans and popes who had it in their power to turn the dream into a reality.

His devotion ravaged his body and his family life. Herzl died at the age of 44 having left behind the blueprint for the emancipation of the Jewish people through a return to national self-determination. His vision combined with his impressive output resulted in the creation of a Zionist weekly newspaper, *Die Welt*, and the literature that would call Jews to action and show them that their liberation was not only urgent but possible. Perhaps most crucially, Herzl had created the architecture that would formally oversee the step-by-step development and implementation of his ideas, the World Zionist Organization, which was founded at the First Zionist Congress.

Theodor Herzl at the Hotel Les Trois Rois in Basel
(E.M. Lilien, Public Domain).

BASEL

The First Zionist Congress opened in Basel, Switzerland on 29 August, 1897. It was an event built in the image of its maker. In implacable Herzlian style, some 200 delegates from 24 countries arrived to the grand casino concert hall of the Stadtcasino Basel, all glamorously attired in black trousers, tails and white ties as if attending the opening of *La Traviata* and not a meeting of continental Jewish leaders.

The grandeur of the occasion was not merely an expression of Herzl's appreciation for the finer things and desire to take for the Jewish national movement, what he saw as the splendor and refinement of Europe. As with everything Herzl did, it had a deeply practical purpose. The event announced the entry of Zionism onto the world stage. It captured the imagination of the press and the public and piqued the interest of European elites. Such an effect could not have been possible had the event been confined to a humble Jewish place of congregation.

Like all of Herzl's achievements, the success of the First Zionist Congress was largely achieved through the inspired labor of Herzl himself. Skepticism abounded but Herzl was able to put on a grand spectacle and to stage an event that no Jewish leader on the continent would have wanted to have been absent from. As one observer noted:

> It was Herzl alone who organized the Congress, all by himself, with his own money and his own labor. . . . He saw to every detail, nothing escaped his attention. There were times when he sat up all night with the students, even addressing envelopes.[5]

The Basel conference established the World Zionist Organization which would be the official body responsible for advancing the Zionist cause. The Jewish people have a bureaucratic streak and are drawn to the orderly. The World Zionist Organization satisfied that and gave an official bearing to Zionism and because of its composition, it was seen as genuinely representative of the Jewish world, which in turn gave its leadership standing to make representations to the press, politicians and diplomats.

An observer to the Third Zionist Congress, held in Basel in 1899, would marvel at the diversity and unity displayed at the gathering, which had brought together all manner of Jew in pursuit of the common purpose of Jewish statehood:

> I looked about me. What Jewish contrasts! A pale-faced Pole with high cheekbones, a German in spectacles, a Russian looking like an angel, a bearded Persian, a clean-shaven American, an Egyptian in a

fez, and over there, that black phantom, towering up in his immense caftan, with his fur cap and pale curls falling from his temples.[6]

During the First Congress, delegates heard reports of the plight of various Jewish communities, giving the proceedings a tragic unifying purpose and a sense of urgency. Statistics were accumulated on population sizes.

The Congress culminated in the adoption of what came to be known as the "Basel Program", a manifesto which succinctly articulated the aims of the Zionist movement, being to "establish a home for the Jewish people in Palestine secured under public law" through "… appropriate means of settlement …" to be achieved by "… strengthening and fostering of Jewish national consciousness [and] the consent of governments."

Herzl was struck by the cohesiveness and sophistication of the Russian delegates at Basel. Viennese Jews were known for sneeringly referring to their eastern brethren as *Ostjuden* (eastern Jews), but here Herzl saw men who, through their scholarly pursuits and bitter experience, truly understood what was needed. The writer Saul Bellow would much later observe the impact that centuries of Tsarist (and, later, Communist) subjugation had on the Jews. "It hardened their minds and matured their souls." Bellow wrote.[7] Herzl had noticed this feature two decades before the Russian Revolution had even occurred.

Aside from the considerable formal business concluded at Basel, the Congress provided an opportunity for mass catharsis, an outpouring of repressed yearning, excitement, anguish and hope.

A particularly compelling moment came when a disagreement between delegates was broken by the entire congress spontaneously joining together to pledge, just as the exiled Jews had pledged in

Babylon nearly 2,500 years earlier, "If I forget thee, O Jerusalem, let my right hand forget its skill."

The opening and closing addresses of Herzl enraptured the audience, drawing a near euphoric feeling of strength and purpose.

The First Zionist Congress had an electrifying effect on the Zionist movement. It completed its transition from the pages of treatises and novels to a movement with devoted adherents ready to take it forward and a clear program ready to be implemented.

Herzl would remark, "At Basel, I founded the Jewish state."

The prominent British-Jewish writer Israel Zangwill characterized Basel like so:

> By the rivers of Babylon we sat down and wept as we remembered Zion. By the river of Basel we sat down and resolved to weep no more.[8]

4

LONDON

By the time of his death in 1904, Theodor Herzl had put the Zionist movement in a state of momentum, with impressive achievements, and a discernible path to its final destination, a Jewish state in Palestine.

Herzl's greatest successes in the years following the First Zionist Congress and the formulation of the Basel Program were in the realm of diplomacy. Herzl believed that the fulfilment of the Zionist dream would be achieved by turning the leaders of the Jewish world towards Zion (which he had largely done at Basel), then winning the support of the wealthiest and most influential Jews in Europe, and in turn persuading the world leaders within whose power it was to grant the Jews their state, to support the Zionist project.

His early efforts to enlist the support of the Rothschild Jewish banking dynasty and Baron Maurice de Hirsch, the German-Jewish financier and philanthropist, had yielded no clear results. Meanwhile, his diplomatic efforts were aimed primarily at the Sultan of Turkey, whose Ottoman Empire had ruled Palestine for four centuries. To get to the sultan, Herzl again fell on what was familiar and sensible to him. He decided that if he convinced the German Kaiser, Wilhelm II of the merits of Zionism, the Kaiser would then intercede on his behalf to his ally the sultan, who would in turn grant the Jews a state in Palestine. But the sultan would not be moved: "When my empire is divided, perhaps [the Jews] will get Palestine for nothing. But only our corpse can be divided."[1] As it happened, the Ottoman Empire was in a terminal state and would be a corpse ripe for division within two decades.

Herzl was relying on a great number of opposing forces to align in his favor. On the one hand, in his dealings with the Kaiser, he was in the company of an avowed antisemite who saw merit in Herzl's proposals not out of a sense of morality or justness but out of the base desire to send the Jews, "the parasites of my empire"[2] to some distant outpost where their harm to German interests could be minimized.

The Russians dealt with Herzl out of a similar calculus: a Jewish homeland meant getting rid of the Jews once and for all. The Russian Interior Minister, Wenzel von Plehve, the consummate antisemite, replied to Herzl upon hearing of his growing movement for a return to Zion: "You are preaching to a convert ... we would very much like to see the creation of an independent Jewish state capable of absorbing several million Jews." It was the more practical version of the "drowning 6 or 7 million Jews" fantasy the Russian Finance Minister Witte had expressed to Herzl.

While the sentiments of stately European antisemites would have at once alarmed and encouraged Herzl, he would soon learn that the cause of Jewish liberation could not be advanced by those motivated by antipathy to the Jewish people. From time to time over the coming decades, Zionist leaders would court or entertain the overtures of antisemites sensing a cold synergy between those wishing to create a new Jewish homeland in Zion and those wishing to reimagine their own homelands free from Jews. These brief and misguided dalliances would be cynically and disingenuously mischaracterized and manipulated by contemporary anti-Zionists eager to falsely characterize the entire movement of Jewish liberation as being in league with racists.

As one driven by romantic idealism as much as pragmatism, Herzl soon grasped that he would have to form alliances with those who truly grasped the necessity, utility and righteousness of a Jewish national rebirth. While his strategy of winning support for Jewish statehood in the corridors of power was the correct one, he came to understand that he was striding the wrong corridors. Herzl soon shifted his focus away from Turkey, Germany and Russia, and looked to Britain.

LONDON

In Britain, Herzl had gradually attained support amongst leading Jewish intellectual and literary figures, most notably the chemist and soon-to-be war hero, Chaim Weizmann and the writer Israel Zangwill. Both Weizmann and Zangwill initially responded to Zionism and Herzl with impeccable British caution, but Basel had shown that both Zionism and Herzl were to be taken seriously and the men were soon ardent supporters of Herzl's single-minded mission.

Aside from being home to numerous Jewish intellectuals who had access to politicians and other members of the British elite, Britain possessed two critical assets from Herzl's point of view.

Firstly, Britain was a world power and an imperial one at that, with vast interests in international affairs across Asia and the Middle East. Secondly, Britain was also home to Nathaniel Mayer Rothschild, the head of the British arm of the Rothschild banking dynasty, whose financial powers placed him close to the center of British capitalism.

Lord Rothschild initially had little time for Herzl's overtures. The epitome of successful integration and privilege, Rothschild hardly required emancipation for himself nor did he see a compelling case for the emancipation of his Jewish kinsmen. But Herzl did not relent and soon world affairs would again conspire against the Jews to reveal the necessity of Zionism before the eyes of the skeptics.

The two Zionist congresses that followed the inaugural event in 1897, were also held in Basel. But sensing the need to capture the hearts and minds of Britain, Herzl decided to stage the Fourth Zionist Congress in London. Addressing the Congress, the largest yet, Herzl declared that it would be "England, mighty England, free England, with its world-embracing outlook, [that] will understand us and our aspirations."

"With England as our starting point," Herzl continued, "we may be sure that the Zionist idea will soar further and higher than ever before."[3]

In Britain, Herzl found a Jewish community deeply divided on the question of Zionism. To the masses of impoverished Jews who had fled the Russian pogroms and settled in the slums and doss houses of Whitechapel, Herzl was a hero, a latter-day Moses who would restore the beleaguered to their Promised Land. But their elected member of parliament, the aristocratic Samuel

Montagu was in turns cordial and suspicious when it came to Herzl and Zionism. Montagu referred to Zionists dismissively as "dreaming a beautiful dream", while also "making a laughing stock of this country."[4]

To cultural figures like Israel Zangwill, Montagu and his ilk were paralyzed in their conservatism, lacked imagination, and were wary of Zionism because it could disrupt their position of privilege and status within British society. Addressing a raucous meeting of Jews in the East End, Zangwill fired at the absence of vision and vigor of the Jewish old-guard: "we are supposed to pray three times a day for the return of Jerusalem but, as soon as we say we want to go back, we are accused of blasphemy."[5]

Meanwhile, Lord Rothschild, whom Herzl was desperately trying to win over through numerous meetings and exchanges of letters, remained steadfastly opposed to the idea of Jewish statehood and a return to Zion. In August 1902, he wrote to Herzl that a Jewish state in Palestine, "would be a ghetto within a ghetto with all the prejudices of a ghetto … [it] would be small and petty, it would be Orthodox and illiberal, and keep out non-Jews and the Christians."[6]

But Lord Rothschild eventually shifted in his position, adopting a stance of cautious support for Zionism.[7] At the same time, the concept of a Jewish national home was beginning to take hold in Britain, well beyond the Jewish community.

Herzl's plan to take the idea of Zionism to the British people by staging the Fourth Zionist Congress there had been a masterstroke. The increasing desperation of Russian Jews caught in the vice of official and popular antisemitism foreshadowed a Jewish refugee crisis hitting Britain. This begged a solution to the question of resettlement of the Russian refugees.

A Royal Commission held in 1902, on which Lord Rothschild served, considered, but ultimately rejected the idea of closing Britain to these desperate eastern Jews, although the flow of Jewish immigrants was ultimately controlled by the passing of the Aliens Act in 1905. These developments brought the prospect of creating an autonomous Jewish state capable of absorbing the refugees, to the forefront of the minds of policy-makers and politicians, including Arthur James Balfour, who was Prime Minister of the United Kingdom from 1902 to 1905.

Many among the British elite also harbored a romantic attachment to the idea of a Jewish return. It not only fulfilled biblical prophecy, it was positively awe-inspiring to contemplate a beleaguered, harried people who stubbornly maintained their unique culture and identity, returning to reclaim and resettle the lands of their forebears some two millennia after their expulsion.

Popular culture and literature gave further texture to the ideal. George Eliot, the most influential novelist of her time had written *Daniel Deronda,* in which an assimilated British Jew learns of his Jewish roots and under the guidance of a sickly, sage-like Jewish elder, rediscovers his Jewish pride and returns to Palestine. Just as the writings of Herzl and his early Zionist contemporaries seared the minds of the Jewish masses and leaders, Eliot did likewise but to the British upper-class that could turn ideas into policies.

KISHINEV

The added petroleum for the advance of the Zionist movement predictably came in the form of a new entry into the annals of human barbarism.

Kishinev, now the capital of Moldova, was at that time a large town in the Bessarabia region of the Russian Empire. There, across two days in April 1903, the Jews were again served a dose of murder, torture, rape and pillage. Dozens were killed. At least 600 Jewish women were raped, many of the perpetrators were known to the victims. Kishinev had followed the familiar formula of newspaper editors, intellectuals and police, stoking popular frustration and base instincts, inflicting callous, needless, unsparing loss and suffering on the Jewish population.

Photos of rows of corpses wrapped in shrouds were published in newspapers around the world, including *The New York Times*. The paper reported on the pogrom as follows:

> The anti-Jewish riots in Kishinev, Bessarabia are worse than the censor will permit to publish. There was a well laid-out plan for the general massacre of Jews on the day following the Orthodox Easter. The mob was led by priests, and the general cry, "Kill the Jews", was taken up all over the city. The Jews were taken wholly unaware and were slaughtered like sheep. The dead number 120 and the injured about 500. The scenes of horror attending this massacre are beyond description. Babies were literally torn to pieces by the frenzied and bloodthirsty mob. The local police made no attempt to check the reign of terror. At sunset the streets were piled with corpses and wounded. Those who could make their escape fled in terror, and the city is now practically deserted of Jews.[8]

An editorial of *The American Hebrew* published shortly after the massacre noted that from Kishinev, "American Zionism had come of age."[9]

In the wake of Kishinev, Christian Zionism matured into an urgent humanitarian concern. "All efforts must be made to establish a Jewish Commonwealth,"[10] was the message delivered by the principal Christian speaker at a Zionist meeting in New York's Cooper Union.

Kishinev also profoundly impacted on how the Jews saw themselves. It was a crippling blow to their sense of worth and esteem. While some reports from Kishinev spoke of gutsy Jewish resistance and attempts at self-defense thwarted by local police who confiscated Jewish arms, the overall image of Kishinev was one of cowering, supine Jews meekly accepting their fate.

The poet Hayim Nahman Bialik, who would become Israel's national poet, was sent to Kishinev after the pogrom by the Jewish community of Odessa. He wrote a damning assessment of Jewish impotence and worse:

> Do not fail to note in the dark corners of Kishinev, crouching husbands, bridegrooms, brothers peering through the cracks of their shelters, watching their wives, sisters, daughters writhing beneath their bestial defilers, suffocating in their own blood, their flesh portioned out as booty.[11]

The accounts of Kishinev inspired feelings of dishonor in international Jewry, coupled with anger and sorrow at the awful fate that had befallen their kin. Eventually the grief subsided but the sense of shame still burned. The pride of the Jewish kings and resistors to Roman and Greek oppression stood in perfect contrast to the animalistic use and disposal of Jewish flesh in Kishinev. Now the Zionist movement took on an even greater redemptive quality. It became a way to stand upright in the face of oppressors. The Zionist writings promising that a national movement and renewed statehood would rebuild Jewish self-esteem were never more resonant. And Kishinev was a mere prologue.

By 1905, mass political upheaval and revolution in Russia was afoot. Russia had just suffered humiliation in the Russo-Japanese war, sailors were rebelling in Kronstadt, and the Tsar's forces massacred demonstrating Russian workers on Bloody Sunday. History has shown that political upheaval, particularly with complex origins and no clear solution, frequently descends into a familiar pounding of Jewish communities for an instant release of frustration or just for good measure.

In Kiev, a city hall meeting held amidst the political chaos, collapsed without resolution. The dissatisfied participants spilled onto the streets and soon embarked on "an orgy of looting, raping, and murder chiefly directed against the factories, the shops, homes, and persons of the Jews."[12]

Over the next two years, pogroms spread through the country resulting in thousands of Jewish deaths. Over 400 were killed in Odessa alone. In some places, the Russian secret police orchestrated the attacks. In others, soldiers and local police actively participated in the crimes.

The 1905 pogroms, sustained and ferocious as they were, turned Zionism into the dominant stream of Jewish political thought and community organizing. It drew on the humanitarian and the religious, notions of justice and equality, and now transcended class and trumped privilege. The argument that good citizenry and integration would alleviate suffering now ran hollow and callous. Zionism was now on the lips not only of the aching Jewish corpus, but of Britain's leading men – Winston Churchill, David Lloyd George and Arthur Balfour.

After seeing Kishinev, the poet Bialik wrote his epic poem, *"The City of Slaughter,"* which included the lines:

Tomorrow the rain will wash their mingled blood
Into the runners, and it will be lost
In rubbish heap, in stagnant pool, in mud.
Its cry will not be heard.
It will descend into the deep, or water the cockle-burr.
And all things will be as they ever were.[13]

But the blood and pain was too heavy and deep to ignore. After Kishinev and the pogroms of 1905, things could never be as they ever were.

Aftermath of the Kishinev Pogrom (Public Domain).

5

CHEMISTRY

Herzl had successfully re-orientated the political thrust of Zionism from western and central Europe to Britain, where the future of the Middle East would soon be decided.

Herzl could not have known that the 400-year grip of the Ottoman Empire on the Middle East would be released in a matter of years or that unlike in Germany and Russia, where any official support for Zionism was based on sinister motives, Britain's ruling class contained true believers in the cause of Jewish national return. But Herzl was able to distinguish the dead-ends from the opportunities. The resulting success could in large part be attributed to Herzl's vision and Herculean appetite for toil, and the sweep of world affairs over which Herzl had no influence.

Quite apart from the official diplomatic efforts to achieve a Jewish national home, the practical fulfilment of Zionism through Jewish migration and development of the land, was rumbling along. The Zionist writers and thinkers had stirred the desire to return that lay dormant in the hearts and minds of the Jewish masses, and had articulated that such a return was both possible and necessary to save the Jewish people from external enemies and their internal malaise.

The early migrants came predominantly from those places where the hatred was at its hottest – Russia and Romania, and also Yemen. These migrants were the vanguard, the pioneers that would prepare the land and construct the institutions that would eventually form the pillars of the new state – defense, organized labor, a press, cultural and educational institutions, and government.

Jewish philanthropy enabled the acquisition of sites for universities, the founding of schools, vineyards and art academies. The Jewish National Fund, the formation of which was foreshadowed by Herzl at the First Zionist Congress in Basel and formally established at the Fifth Congress held in 1901, would serve as the primary charitable vehicle which allowed the Jewish settlers to lawfully purchase land, often at inflated prices, for homes and institutions. On the road from Jaffa to Jerusalem, the village of Ben Shemen was founded to give a home for the orphans of Kishinev.

In 1909, Deganya, the first communal farm or *kibbutz*, was established on the land following experimentation in collective farming and land reclamation. Its model of shared ownership of the means of production and equal distribution of the produce and proceeds of sale among the farmers would soon be replicated throughout the land, forming the backbone of the pre-state society's agriculture. The kibbutz also instilled a belief in collective toil and shared duties, a lusty appreciation of the land, and fostered early autonomy and responsibility for the youth, a welcome respite from the fretting parenting of European Jewry.

These values would contribute immensely to the bourgeoning society. Not only in terms of production and enterprise, but in creating a new Jewish spirit and ethos reconnected to the historic hillocks and valleys of Palestine, joyous of physical labor and full of the hearty pride that comes from working a cherished land.

Also in 1909, Tel Aviv (meaning "Hill of Spring"), which would eventually become the financial capital of the nation, was founded on sand dunes just outside the port city of Jaffa, to bring respite from the overcrowded warrens and recalcitrant landlords that made life in Jaffa stifling.

The land on which Tel Aviv was founded was also acquired by the Jewish National Fund, and registered in the name of a Dutch national, Jacobus Kann, to circumvent Ottoman laws that forbade land purchases by individual Jews.[1] 66 founding families that had formed a building society known as Ahuzat Bayit (*homestead*), gathered on the dunes clutching twice their number in sea-shells, for a lottery draw that would see families paired with plots of land. The process by which the new city was founded, part methodical, part whimsical, was indicative of how Jewish settlers were practically realizing the Zionist vision. They were finding ways to overcome obstacles, and through small, unified endeavors, they were gradually completing a grand project.

But the ultimate goal, the return to Jewish independence and the reconstitution of a Jewish state in the land, could not be achieved merely through organic migration and land acquisition. It demanded securing official recognition of the legitimacy of the Zionist project and the grant of the right to self-govern by the sovereign of the land.

The local activities of the Jews were also being undermined by the Ottomans who were intent on suppressing any activities that might challenge the Empire's control of the land and lead to its eventual decolonization. The Ottoman authorities were adamant that no ethnic group in Palestine should become too prosperous or too assertive. All the while they harshly suppressed any nationalistic feeling that might pose a challenge to its rule. The Ottomans were playing a dangerous game, one that never ends well for colonial rulers seeking to subjugate local peoples with nowhere to go and nothing to lose. The British would soon be trying their hand at the same hopeless pursuit.

With increased Jewish ownership of land and political organization, the hostility of the local Arabs was also aroused. Local Arab politicians campaigned on platforms vowing to keep the Jews in a state of subservience and to limit further Jewish migration. This feeling soon received official sanction as Constantinople would decree in the summer of 1914 that Jews living outside the Ottoman Empire could not settle in Palestine. The announcement came just as the Jews of Russia were facing fresh waves of violence following another infamous accusation of Jewish ritual murder of a Christian child in what came to be known as the Beilis Affair. The Ottoman policy of barring Jewish migration was then escalated upon the outbreak of the First World War. Eighteen thousand Jews from Palestine were expelled.

The allocation of land through the drawing of lots by members of the building society that founded Tel Aviv in 1909 (Avraham Soskin, Public Domain).

WEIZMANN

Back in London, the official Zionist campaign stood on the threshold of a momentous achievement.

In 1904, the year of Herzl's sudden and premature death, Chaim Weizmann, a 30-year-old chemist, born in a village in the Russian Empire and educated in Germany and Switzerland, accepted an offer to lecture in organic chemistry at the University of Manchester. Weizmann's movements from Russia to Western Europe and finally Britain, resembled the journey of modern Zionism itself. If Leon Pinsker represented the anguished cry of the millions of Jews under the lash of the Tsar and his pogromists, and Herzl stood for the path of practical diplomacy and organization that could alleviate their suffering, then the chemist, Weizmann was the next catalyst, who would build upon the achievements of his forebears and deliver official recognition of the right of the Jews to return to Zion.

Weizmann was a delegate to the Second Zionist Congress in 1898, and had described the ascent of Herzl and the ideas he professed to be a "bolt from the blue".[2]

Unlike Herzl, Weizmann intimately knew and understood the eastern Jews, whose condition was most acute, and largely in whose aid the Zionist movement was progressing with great urgency. Whereas Herzl was in many ways an atypical Jew in his estrangement from Jewish custom, religious observance, and his heavy assimilation into broader European society, Weizmann remained a Jew's Jew, able to present a certain authenticity when engaging with British leaders and to invoke a feeling of fraternity among other Jews. Where Herzl's frenzied sense of purpose and soaring oratory elicited feelings of being in the presence of the near-messianic, Weizmann was described as "the leader in whom the vast majority of Jews saw a model of their own virtues and moral attributes."[3]

He stood with Russian Jewry in opposing any proposal for forming a Jewish national home outside Palestine, and was generally seen as an ideal conduit between the ideas and feelings of the Eastern European Jews and those of Western European Jewry.

Isaiah Berlin, who was a close friend of Weizmann's wrote of him: "In the realm of action, the great man seems able, almost alone and singlehanded, to transform one form of life into another..."[4]

Weizmann's capacity to transform made him a worthy

successor to Herzl. Herzl's enigmatic, romantic qualities had turned something as amorphous and fanciful as the ingathering and rehabilitation of an ancient people, into the realm of real plans, real action and real outcomes. He had rallied the Jewish masses, inspired their leaders to believe that Zionism could be fulfilled, and put the Zionist project into locomotion. Now Weizmann, with his studious, measured, patient and pragmatic nature would soon convert Herzl's enormous achievements into a tangible diplomatic and political result. Herzl was the man for his time and Weizmann was the man for his. Herzl performed his act of transformation in immaculate evening dress in the grand casino concert hall of the Stadtcasino Basel. Weizmann would perform his in a laboratory coat in Manchester.

Chaim Weizmann (Government Press Office, Israel, Creative Commons).

ACETONE

In the years between his commencing at the University of Manchester and the beginning of the Great War in 1914, Weizmann combined his political activities in aid of Zionism with his scientific research. In particular, he had been enlisted by more senior colleagues to assist in research on the production of synthetic rubber, which would have a major industrial application.

Weizmann's experimentation with butanol in the production of synthetic rubber did not immediately bear fruit, but it did lead him to discover a process for the large-scale production of acetone.

The significance of Weizmann's discovery did not immediately dawn on him but it was soon made apparent to Weizmann by more commercially-minded counterparts. When gunpowder is mixed with acetone during the production process, it has the effect of greatly reducing the smoke released when the gunpowder is ignited. The military implications of this were enormous, particularly to the Royal Navy. It meant that British soldiers and seamen could fire heavy guns without revealing their positions. Weizmann's discovery of a method for mass-producing acetone would have a major impact on military strategy, and with it, the very outcome of the First World War.

Weizmann's discovery and its centrality to the British naval campaign soon put him in the company of the First Lord of the Admiralty, Winston Churchill. With no time to waste, Churchill put it to Weizmann frankly, "Well Dr Weizmann, we need thirty thousand tons of acetone. Can you make it?"[5] Weizmann's answer satisfied Churchill and the former was commissioned by the British Government to begin work without delay. His trials exceeded expectations and by February 1917, British distilleries were producing hundreds of tons of acetone a month using Weizmann's recipe.

There was something of the wisdom of Jeremiah in the service of Weizmann to the British realm. He had truly sought the welfare of the land where he had been sent into exile, and in its welfare, he found his own.

Weizmann did not attain the sort of material wealth from his discoveries that one would expect. Indeed, when he was first commissioned by the government to begin work solving the problem of the acetone shortage, he proposed to forego payment completely.[6] But Weizmann had rendered an enormous service to the British Empire in its time of great need and this would not quickly be forgotten.

David Lloyd George dealt much with Weizmann during the war in his capacity first as Chancellor of the Exchequer, then as Minister for Munitions, then as Secretary of State for War, and finally as Prime Minister. He reveals in his war memoirs just how significantly Weizmann's patriotism and national service impacted on the course of Zionism.

Lloyd George recalls that upon hearing of Weizmann's solving the acetone shortage, he turned to Weizmann and said:

> You have rendered a great service to the State and I should like to ask the Prime Minister [Lloyd George was still Minister for Munitions then] to recommend you to his Majesty for some honour.

Weizmann is said to have replied, "There is nothing I want for myself."

Lloyd George pressed, "But is there nothing we can do as a recognition of your valuable assistance to the country?"

Weizmann then delivered his request: "Yes, I would like you to do something for my people."

That "something" for Weizmann's people came in the form of a letter written by the Foreign Secretary Lord Arthur Balfour addressed to Lord Lionel Walter Rothschild, known as the "Balfour Declaration", which for the first time authoritatively expressed British support for the establishment of a Jewish national home in Palestine.

Lloyd George wrote that his conversation with Weizmann, "was the fount and origin of the famous declaration about the National Home for Jews in Palestine."[7]

Whether the conversation Lloyd George recounted in his memoirs in fact took place in the way that he recorded it, or indeed whether it took place at all, is a matter of conjecture. What is clear is that Britain felt a great debt to Chaim Weizmann, the Zionist leader whose diligence, intellect, and sense of civic duty had made a significant contribution to Britain's military effort at a critical juncture of the war.

Of course, such a feeling would not have led Britain to act against its interests or to do something it wasn't already minded to do. In addition to assessing that a Jewish state in Palestine formed under British patronage and protection would serve as a key ally in a key region, the British may have privately assessed that promising the establishment of a Jewish home in Palestine upon the defeat of Germany and the Ottomans in the Great War, would entice American Jewry to lobby for American entry into the War, something the British certainly favored.[8] Yet it is difficult to see how such a view, founded as it is in a rather tenuous, dubious overestimation of Jewish influence on international affairs, could have played a major part in the policy-making of the time.

The impact of Weizmann's war service on the course of Zionism should not be underestimated. As Jehuda Reinharz observed, "the men at Whitehall and in Downing Street who had placed their faith in Weizmann the scientist to solve a problem of national magnitude were easily persuaded to extend the same support to Weizmann the Zionist politician."[9]

Significant as Weizmann's war efforts undeniably were, the support for Zionism among British statesmen did not pour out of Weizmann's barrels of acetone. As Weizmann observed in his own memoirs, "those British statesmen of the old school ... understood as a reality the concept of return. It appealed to their tradition and their faith."[10]

A further factor that was critical to the issuing of the Balfour Declaration was Weizmann's ability to forge vital personal connections.

Chaim and Vera Weizmann (left) with David Lloyd George (3rd from right) and Herbert Samuel (center) (The David B. Keidan Collection of Digital Images from the Central Zionist Archives, via Harvard University Library).

SCOTT

One particularly fateful meeting to the story of Zionism, came in September 1914 after something as trivial as an invitation to Weizmann to take tea at the home of a fellow Jew of Manchester. There, Weizmann made the acquaintance of a highly influential member of the liberal gentry, Charles Prestwich (C.P.) Scott, the editor and publisher of the *Manchester Guardian* newspaper (later the *Guardian*), and a former member of the British parliament. Weizmann and Scott struck up a conversation which quickly turned to Weizmann's national origins and his belief in a Jewish homeland. The two men quickly became friends and Scott would eventually write to a friend and journalist at his paper, Harry Sacher, himself a Jew and a committed Zionist, of the impact that Weizmann had had on him:

> I have had several conversations with Dr Weizmann on the Jewish question and he has, I think, opened his whole mind to me. I found him extraordinarily interesting – a rare combination of the idealism and the severely practical which are the two essentials of statesmanship … What struck me in his view was first the perfectly clear conception of Jewish nationalism – an intense and burning sense of the Jew as Jew … and secondly, arising out of that, necessary for its satisfaction and development, his demand for a country, a homeland, which for him, and for anyone sharing his view of Jewish nationality, could only be the ancient home of his race.[11]

Weizmann's relationship with Scott not only secured the support of a highly influential person in his own right, it led to an introduction, at Scott's insistence, to David Lloyd George. The relationship with Lloyd George would be deepened during the years of Weizmann's work with acetone, during which Scott intervened personally on a number of occasions to vouch for Weizmann's good character and ensure that Weizmann received due recognition for his efforts. In particular, Scott intervened at times when he feared that Weizmann's Jewishness had led to suspicions about his loyalty to Britain.

Weizmann's relationship with Scott, and in turn Lloyd George, demonstrates the central role played by personal contact and persuasion to policy-making. It shows the critical importance of skilled advocates capable of striking friendships and leaving an impression on those possessed of real power. Herzl of course had understood this too and had labored intensively to develop relationships which he could then leverage into political outcomes.

When Lloyd George became Prime Minister in December 1916, he installed Arthur Balfour as his Foreign Secretary.

Weizmann had met Balfour through a mutual friend, the philosopher, Samuel Alexander. Upon discussing Jewish nationhood and a return to Zion with Weizmann, Balfour recounted that he was "moved to tears". "It is not a dream," Balfour said of the idea of a Jewish national return following a meeting with Weizmann, "it is a great cause and I understand it".[12]

Weizmann's sense of enterprise, his brilliance as a scientist and a statesman, and his ability to impact those he was fated to meet, were of enormous service to the cause of Zionism.

As the Ottoman grip on Palestine was slipping and the Middle-East would soon be remade by the victorious Allied Powers, Balfour was about to put pen to paper on a document that Isaiah Berlin considered the "the greatest event in Jewish history since the destruction of Judea."[13]

> Foreign Office,
> November 2nd, 1917.
>
> Dear Lord Rothschild,
>
> I have much pleasure in conveying to you, on behalf of His Majesty's Government, the following declaration of sympathy with Jewish Zionist aspirations which has been submitted to, and approved by, the Cabinet
>
> "His Majesty's Government view with favour the establishment in Palestine of a national home for the Jewish people, and will use their best endeavours to facilitate the achievement of this object, it being clearly understood that nothing shall be done which may prejudice the civil and religious rights of existing non-Jewish communities in Palestine, or the rights and political status enjoyed by Jews in any other country"
>
> I should be grateful if you would bring this declaration to the knowledge of the Zionist Federation.
>
> *[signature: Arthur James Balfour]*

The Balfour Declaration.

6

BALFOUR'S NOTE

The Balfour Declaration was a brief letter, written by the Foreign Secretary in Lloyd George's government, Arthur Balfour, in which Balfour conveyed to Lord Lionel Walter Rothschild, the decision of the Cabinet on the question of a Jewish national home in Palestine.

The substantive part of the letter, the Declaration itself, is a mere 67 words. They do not immediately strike one as being momentous, life-altering words. These are the words of tepid, diplomatic language, deliberately vague in certain respects and carefully carving out rights and limiting obligations. But the Declaration was of critical importance to the cause of Zionism.

It stood, not only as official British recognition of the Jewish people's claim to Palestine, and the Jewish desire to establish a new national home in the land, but as a pledge by the British Government to actively work to establish such a home. In this way, the Balfour Declaration made Britain a critical actor and ally in the fulfilment of Zionism.

At Weizmann's suggestion, the letter was addressed to Lord Rothschild. Weizmann records in his memoirs that when Balfour asked to whom the declaration should be addressed, he suggested it be Rothschild "rather than myself, though I was the President of the English Zionist Federation."[1]

The letter states that the matter of a Jewish national home had been considered by the Cabinet (the deliberations took place on October 31, 1917) with the conclusion of Cabinet on the issue being a "declaration of sympathy with Jewish Zionist aspirations". The letter then makes the two key undertakings by the British Government to Rothschild and the Zionist Federation, as representatives of the Zionist cause:

> His Majesty's Government view with favor the establishment in Palestine of a national home for the Jewish people, and will use their best endeavors to facilitate the achievement of this object.[2]

The letter further stipulated that, "nothing shall be done which may prejudice the civil and religious rights of the existing non-Jewish communities in Palestine, or the rights and political status enjoyed by Jews in any other country." This important qualifying statement at once addressed the concerns and affirmed the rights of non-Jews in Palestine and of Jews who feared that Zionism and the establishment of a national home could undermine their ability to continue living freely as citizens of other states.

Speaking in the centenary year of the Declaration, the Fourth Lord Rothschild, Jacob, called the letter addressed to his cousin, 'the greatest event in Jewish life for thousands of years, a miracle ...'[3]

The jurist, Ruth Lapidoth considered the Balfour Declaration to be more than a mere statement of support for Zionism, but "a legally binding document", based on the certainty of the undertakings contained in the Declaration, being to "use best endeavors" to achieve the establishment of a Jewish national home in Palestine, and the intention of the British Government that the document should be binding, as evidenced by, among other things, the fact that it was made in writing and issued by the Foreign Secretary.[4]

Whether or not the terms of the Declaration immediately had legal force or attained it in future years through international agreements into which those terms were incorporated, the Declaration was easily the greatest accomplishment of Zionism to that time, and had decisively, irrevocably placed the Jews on a path home.

Lord Jacob Rothschild, again in his centenary reflections, assessed the origins of the Declaration and Weizmann's role in it:

> It was the most incredible piece of opportunism. You had an impoverished would-be scientist, Chaim Weizmann, who somehow gets to England, meets a few people, including members of my family, seduces them, he has such charm and conviction, he gets to Balfour, and unbelievably, he persuades Lord Balfour, and Lloyd George, the prime minister, and most of the ministers, that this idea of a national home for Jews should be allowed to take place. I mean it's so, so unlikely.[5]

Rothschild was correct in seeing the wondrous way in which the Declaration came about. But Balfour's letter was not the product of pure chance or happy chaos as Rothschild implies. It was the culmination of painstaking efforts and enormous toil. It was not merely a case of Weizmann wooing a few key men in Her Majesty's Government. One can identify a continuum from the writings of the early Zionists in Russia to the cobblestoned courtyard of Paris's École Militaire where Herzl witnessed the degradation of Dreyfus, to the shuttle diplomacy of Herzl and community organizing resulting in the First Zionist Congress in Basel, to the decision to stage the Fourth Zionist Congress in London,

Weizmann's work in Zionism and his war contribution, and finally the Balfour letter itself.

But as in every major development in the story of Zionism, this particular success was achieved partly through toil, vision and the ability to seize the day, and partly as a result of major global events over which the Zionists had no control whatsoever.

On 31 October 1917, British and Dominion forces attacked and captured their first city inside Palestine. While units of the 20th British Infantry Corps and Yeomanry Mounted Division attacked Beersheba from the south and west, 800 bayonet-wielding horsemen of the 4th Australian Light Horse Brigade charged from the east across a five kilometer plain and over-ran Turkish defenses. Beersheba was captured. That same day, the British War Cabinet authorized a declaration of sympathy for Zionist aspirations to be made by Foreign Secretary Arthur Balfour. The Balfour Declaration was published two days later.

The victory at Beersheba was the first of a series of British successes that brought about the collapse of Ottoman rule in Palestine ten months later, thereby creating the opportunity for the British to chart a new course in the land.

A week after the fall of Beersheba, Gaza fell also. On 9 December 1917, Jerusalem fell to the British. Haifa, another position of immense strategic importance with its seaport and rail lines heading to the east, would eventually fall to Britain's Indian lancers on September 23 of the following year, after another spirited cavalry charge.

In a further instance of serendipity, 12,000 of the 18,000 Jews expelled from Palestine at the outbreak of World War I by the

Turkish authorities, had arrived in the northern Egyptian city of Alexandria by boat in December 1914. They took refuge among the ancient Jewish community there. It was also in Alexandria that the Jewish expellees encountered troops of the Australia and New Zealand Army Corps (ANZACs), newly arrived by convoy via the Suez Canal.

Among the exiled Jews in Alexandria were Vladimir (later Ze'ev) Jabotinsky and Joseph Trumpeldor, who would impress upon the Allied soldiers the virtues of creating a Jewish battalion to join the war effort against the Turks. The Zion Mule Corps was formed in Alexandria in March 1915 by Jabotinsky and Trumpeldor, and served under the command of the British. 562 Jewish men of the Zion Mule Corps sailed from Egypt to the Dardanelles to fight alongside Allied forces in one of the bloodiest campaigns of the War.[6] Half of them served with distinction alongside other British forces at Cape Helles. The other half served with the Anzacs at Gallipoli for several weeks. Although they were a small unit who would carry ammunition, water and bully beef to British and Dominion soldiers, they became a symbol of courage, spending eight months under fire with no shelter, bringing critical supplies to their British comrades.

The Jewish forces were placed under the command of a British officer, John Henry Patterson who noted their heroism:

> Many of the Zionists whom I thought somewhat lacking in courage showed themselves fearless to a degree when under heavy fire, while Captain Trumpeldor actually reveled in it, and the hotter it became the more he liked it ...[7]

Patterson developed a deep regard for Trumpeldor and Jabotinsky. In much the same way as Weizmann's personal qualities impacted on how Lloyd George and Balfour came to view the cause that was central to Weizmann's endeavors and identity, when Patterson saw Jewish national hopes embodied in vigorous and courageous men, he became a life-long devotee of Zionism.

The great Israeli historian and father of Benjamin Netanyahu, Benzion Netanyahu, made Patterson godfather to his first son, and named the boy, "Yonatan", in honor of Patterson.[8] Yonatan would mature into a war hero himself, falling in battle in a daring commando raid at Entebbe in 1976.

The Zion Mules Corps was considered the first regular Jewish fighting force since Simon Bar Kokhba led the Jewish revolt against the brutal regime of the Emperor Hadrian.[9] It served a distinct purpose in the shaping of a new Jewish identity and self-conception. Patterson had been surprised by the fighting qualities of bespectacled, bookish Jews, who would have seemed to lack the robust qualities one associates with a warrior. But the exceptional valor of these men set an example to the Jewish masses. Just as the early pioneer settlers to Palestine showed the joy that could come from swapping urban trappings for humbly attending the soil of treasured lands, the fighting Jews at the Dardanelles showed that this perennially oppressed nation of perceived neurotic weaklings obediently awaiting the next lash of the antisemite, could in fact stand tall and fight.

WILSON

While the Zionists had certainly impressed the British through the industry of Weizmann and the spirit of Trumpeldor and Jabotinsky, the Declaration that came from the Foreign Secretary was not a unilateral act of gratitude. Foreign policy and post-war reconstruction are not conducted in such a way.

The Balfour Declaration was consistent with an earlier statement by the French Foreign Minister, Jules Cambon expressing sympathy for a Jewish national home. Cambon called it "the renaissance of the Jewish nationality in that Land from which the people of Israel were exiled so many centuries ago."[10]

A few months after the Balfour letter, US President Woodrow Wilson outlined his own vision for peacemaking and a postwar settlement to the US Congress. Wilson presented his "fourteen points", within which the Balfour Declaration would cozily fit. Wilson affirmed the right of self-determination, calling on nations to "determine [their] own institutions", and demanding that non-Turkish nationalities "… now under Turkish rule should be assured an undoubted security of life and an absolutely unmolested opportunity of autonomous development …"[11]

Wilson also called for the founding of "a general association of nations formed under specific covenants for the purpose of affording mutual guarantees of political independence and territorial integrity …"[12]

The next step in building international consensus around the idea of a Jewish national home in Palestine, was to explicitly apply Wilson's support for the peoples living in the former lands of the Ottoman Empire attaining "autonomous development", to the Jews and to Palestine.

Like his Christian coreligionists across the Atlantic, Wilson had an ideological and emotional connection to the idea of the ancient people of the book, restoring their national sovereignty and esteem, and again taking their place among the nations of the world. He also had close Jewish acquaintances of high eminence who could impress upon the President the nobility and practical benefits of allowing the Jews to reclaim their homeland. The primary interlocutors to the President in support of Zionism were Louis D. Brandeis, who on Wilson's nomination in 1916, became the first Jew to serve on the US Supreme Court; Felix Frankfurter, another jurist who would later be appointed to the Supreme Court by Franklin D. Roosevelt; and Rabbi Stephen S. Wise, whose involvement with Zionism dated back to the Second Zionist Congress held in Basel in 1898.

Brandeis, Frankfurter and Wise faced the formidable task of convincing the President to maintain his support for the Zionist cause in the face of a growing tide of State Department hostility and increasingly organized opposition to Zionism. This opposition emanated from a combination of Arab nationalists, Christian antisemites, and assimilationist Jews concerned, much like the British Jewish gentry, about keeping their privileged positions in society undisturbed.

Wilson gave an eventual nod of support for the Balfour Declaration in the form of a delicately-worded letter written by the President to Rabbi Wise that stated that the President "... had watched the progress of the Zionist Commission in Palestine with much interest ... and welcomed the opportunity to express his satisfaction with the progress of the movement since the Balfour Declaration and noted with approval that even in such time of crisis, the cornerstone of Hebrew University [in Jerusalem] had been laid.[13]

The letter was greeted with jubilation by Jewish groups around the world. Wilson's public support for the Balfour Declaration was a vital endorsement just as the postwar conferences, during which the future of Palestine would be decided, were to begin.

LETTERS

The official support of the President of the United States also gave a degree of clarity to the future of Palestine at a time when the British and French were making often ambiguous, possibly contradictory, promises to rival claimants to the land.

In 1915-16, there had been an exchange of letters between the British High Commissioner in Egypt, Sir Henry McMahon, and the grand Sharif of Mecca, Hussein ibn Ali, which came to be known as the McMahon-Hussein Correspondence. The correspondence sought to secure Arab support for the Allied war effort in the Middle East in exchange for promises of sovereign Arab rule once the Ottomans were defeated. It was now being argued by the Arabs that McMahon's promises to the Arabs included Palestine. The weight of serious analysis, however, suggests that the correspondence never covered Palestine.

In 1922, Winston Churchill considered it to be settled that "the whole of Palestine west of the Jordan [river] was excluded from Sir Henry McMahon's pledge."[14] McMahon himself, writing in the *Times of London* in 1937, sought to settle the matter once and for all:

> I feel it is my duty to state, and I do so definitely and emphatically, that it was not intended by me in giving this pledge to King Hussein to include Palestine in the area in which Arab independence was promised. I also had every reason to believe at the time that the fact that Palestine was not included in my

pledge was well understood by King Hussein."¹⁵

In fact, Hussein seemed so comfortable with the idea of the Jews being granted a small portion of the Middle East so long as the Arabs could exercise self-determination everywhere else, that he wrote an article asking the Palestinian Arabs to welcome the Jews.¹⁶ Hussein's article, published on March 23, 1918, in *Al Qibla*, the daily newspaper of Mecca, affirmed that Palestine was "a sacred and beloved homeland of its original sons," (the Jews), and that "the return of these exiles to their homeland will prove materially and spiritually an experimental school for their [Arab] brethren." He called on the Arab population in Palestine to welcome the Jews and to cooperate with them for their common welfare.¹⁷

Chaim Weizmann had been busy too. He was able to secure an agreement with Hussein's son, Amir Faisal dated January 3, 1919 that confirmed Faisal's support for Zionist aspirations and the Balfour Declaration, including further Jewish migration, in exchange for a pledge by the Zionists to preserve Islamic places of worship, and to assist the local Arabs in development of the land. Faisal added a handwritten caveat to the effect that the agreement would be null and void if the British promise to the Arabs of independence elsewhere in the Middle East went unfulfilled, further indicating that the Arab leaders were always prepared to do without Palestine as long as their far grander territorial ambitions were met.

Weizmann meets with Amir Faisal. The two would sign the Weizmann-Faisal agreement that confirmed Faisal's support for Zionist aspirations and the Balfour Declaration, (Public Domain).

PARIS

On January 18, 1919, with the Ottoman Empire, Austro-Hungary and Germany defeated, the victors of World War I met at the Palace of Versailles outside Paris to determine the terms of peace and ordain a new international system to keep the world from further war.

While the future of the erstwhile lands of the vanquished Ottoman Empire were critical to Zionism, the main event of the Conference was the Treaty of Versailles and an imposed settlement on Germany. As history would unfold, it would be the Treaty of Versailles that would have the profoundest effect on Jewish history. Its punitive conditions sought to impose a collective sense of war guilt and shame on the German people in the belief that demoralizing Germany would keep her from further war. But this only created the resentment and sense of grievance in which Hitler could ascend.

For the Zionist leadership, the Paris Conference presented the opportunity to enshrine the Jewish claim to the land into international law.

The Jews had stood on the correct side of history by contributing to the Allied victory. The Balfour Declaration was a clear and authoritative pledge to facilitate Jewish migration to the land and expressed support for the eventual creation of a new Jewish homeland. Subsequent diplomatic efforts had widened the support for Zionism from Britain to the US and even had a measure of support from parts of the Arab world where it was believed that a conciliatory approach on Palestine would grease the wheels on the process of Arab independence elsewhere. Now the Zionist delegation to Paris sought to bundle these diplomatic achievements and turn them into international recognition of Jewish national rights.

The US proposal for Palestine put forward during the deliberations at Paris broadly reflected the Balfour Declaration. The US "… recommended that there be established a separate state of Palestine" … and that this state should be recognized "as a Jewish state as soon as it is a Jewish state in fact."[18]

The proposal further said of the Jews and Palestine: "It was the cradle and home of their vital race, which has made large spiritual contributions to mankind, and is the only land in which they can hope to find a home of their own; they being in this last respect unique among significant peoples."[19]

LEAGUE OF NATIONS

From Paris came a new global architecture in the form of the League of Nations, the forerunner to the United Nations. Signed in the summer of 1919, the charter of the League of Nations spoke of a determination to "promote international co-operation and to achieve international peace and security," by a commitment to avoid war, and a system of collective security which would lead to the peaceful resolution of disputes through the mechanisms of the League, and by "scrupulous respect for all treaty obligations".[20]

As to the question of what was to become of the former colonies of the Ottoman Empire, including Palestine, the 32 original members of the League of Nations addressed this in Article 22 of the League's Covenant. It was determined that as to the former colonies inhabited "…by peoples not yet able to stand by themselves under the strenuous conditions of the modern world … there should be applied the principle that the well-being and development of such peoples form a sacred trust of civilization…"

This "trust" took the form of the mandatory system, by which the "advanced nations" (known as the "Mandatories") would take temporary responsibility over the former colonies "on behalf of the League", and render practical assistance to the native peoples of these lands "… until such time as they are able to stand alone."[21]

In this way, the founding document of the League of Nations sought to give practical effect and international agreement to the peace-making vision of Woodrow Wilson, specifically, his desire to see the former lands of the Ottoman Empire decolonized to allow "absolutely unmolested opportunity of autonomous development".[22]

With the League of Nations covenant signed and the mandatory system in place, the following year, the Allied Powers reconvened, this time at San Remo in Italy to begin signing the treaties, the "scrupulous respect" for which, would be the basis of peace and security.

At the Paris Conference the previous year, the Zionist delegation headed by Chaim Weizmann addressed the conference, pressing the claim for a Jewish state in Palestine. But it was the address of another Zionist leader, Menachem Ussishkin that most impacted the conference and stated the case for Zionism with the fusion of intellect and idealism by which Zionism had been defined. Ussishkin captured the yearning, the sorrow, the injustice that had marked the period of exile of the Jews. He also demonstrated the new fortitude of an old people, a determination to stand upright and claim what they held to be inalienably theirs. He spoke as Bialik the poet and Weizmann the chemist.

> Nowhere have we found rest for our weary spirit nor for our aching feet. Persecution, expulsion, cruel riots, unbroken distress – such have been our lot during all these generations in all the countries of the world, and in these very days – when the wielders of all the world's destiny have proclaimed the liberation of the nations, the equality of the nations, and the self-determination of every separate nation – Russian Jewry, which I represent here, is undergoing fresh torrents of murder and rioting the like of which were never known even in the Middle Ages.
>
> For us there is no way out save to receive, under your authority and subject to your supervision, one secure place in the world where we shall be able to renew our own lives and revive the national and cultural tradition which has come down to us from ancient times, and where can that secure spot be save in our historic country?[23]

In April 1920, the great powers to which Ussishkin appealed on behalf of the Jewish masses, would assemble at Villa Devachan on a hillside overlooking the Italian Riviera town of San Remo. There they would determine whether this era of liberation would extend to the Jewish people and whether the promises made to the Jews in the throes of the Great War would be honored.

Delegates to the San Remo conference in Italy, April 1920 (Wikimedia Commons).

SAN REMO

The meeting of British Prime Minister David Lloyd George, Alexandre Mitterrand of France, Francesco Nitti of Italy and Japan's Keishiro Matsui at San Remo produced a Resolution on Palestine that finally made it possible, under the watch of Britain, for the Jews to return to the land from which they had been expelled nearly two millennia before, and to reconstruct the institutions of free and independent government.

The Resolution placed Palestine in the hands of a "mandatory", determined to be Britain, which would act on behalf of the League of Nations in preparing the land for independence pursuant to Article 22 of the League of Nations Covenant. But the Resolution went further. It charged Britain with responsibility for "... putting into effect the declaration ... by the British Government, and adopted by the other Allied Powers, in favor of the establishment in Palestine of a national home for the Jewish people, it being clearly understood that nothing shall be done which may prejudice the civil and religious rights of existing non-Jewish communities in Palestine, or the rights and political status enjoyed by Jews in any other country."

The Resolution had done exactly what the Zionist leadership had hoped for since Lord Balfour's note to Rothschild in November 1917. It took the pledges contained in the letter and gave them the force and legitimacy of international law.

Now that it was determined that the British would be granted a mandate to administer Palestine in readiness for Jewish statehood, the precise terms of that mandate were set out in a further agreement which was formally adopted by the League of Nations on 24 July 1922, and which took effect the following year.

THE MANDATE

The League of Nations Mandate for Palestine gave formal "recognition to the historical connection of the Jewish people with Palestine and to the grounds for reconstituting their national home in that country". It made Britain responsible for "placing the country under such political, administrative and economic conditions as will secure the establishment of the Jewish national home" (Article 2); and to "facilitate Jewish immigration under suitable conditions and shall encourage ... close settlement by Jews, on the land, including State lands and waste lands not required for public purposes (Article 6)."[24]

At Paris, Woodrow Wilson had noted that despite their ancient connection to the land, owing to forcible depopulation, the Jews amounted to "barely a sixth of the total population of 700,000 in Palestine ..."[25] The obligation on the British to facilitate settlement of the land by Jews was therefore central to creating the conditions on the ground that would lead to Jewish statehood.

The population of Palestine had long been subject to sharp fluctuations depending on economic conditions elsewhere in the Ottoman Empire and how hospitable Europe was to the Jews at a point in time. Between 1880 and 1919 for example, the Arab population of the coastal city of Haifa, swelled by a factor of 13, as migrant workers seized on new economic opportunities brought about by Jewish migration from Romania and Russia and the new focus on Palestine's economic development following the decline of Ottoman power.[26]

Thousands of Egyptian draft dodgers settled in the land before the Ottoman-Egyptian war of 1831. Some 30,000 Syrians would cross into Palestine during the British Mandate.[27] These movements served to strengthen the hand of the Arabs who could argue that a Jewish state in Palestine would be anathema to the vast majority of the population. Meanwhile, in the first years of the British Mandate, Jewish migration was also picking up steam helped by the end of Ottoman-era restrictions on Jewish migration, Ukrainian inhospitality to the Jews and the passage of antisemitic laws in Poland in the 1920s.

Shifting demographics and rapid land acquisitions set against the backdrop of the post-war reconstruction, served to heighten tensions between the Arabs and Jews in Palestine. The British would respond by seeking to temporarily soothe one side, then the other, lurching between magnanimity, indifference and harshness while attempting to keep sight of the reason they were in Palestine in the first place – to fulfil the League of Nations Mandate and deliver on the promise of a Jewish national home.

SEVRES

The Arabs for their part, had emerged from the postwar conferences with provisional states in Iraq (also under British stewardship), Syria and Lebanon (both under temporary control of the French). Indeed, the establishment of seven independent Arab states shortly after the end of World War I amply fulfilled the commitments made in the McMahon-Hussein Correspondence.

Four months after San Remo, the Allied Powers met at a porcelain factory in Sevres, France and signed the Treaty of Sevres with the defeated Ottoman Empire. Under the Treaty, Turkey accepted the dismembering of its fallen empire to enable the lands to be administered by the victors in accordance with the League of Nations Covenant and the Paris Peace Conference. While the Treaty was signed but never implemented due to a revolution in Turkey, in part brought on by the onerous terms of the postwar settlement, the Treaty revealed much about Turkish and Arab attitudes to the creation of a Jewish state in Palestine at that time.

Article 95 again incorporated the precise wording of the Balfour Declaration on the establishment of a Jewish homeland in Palestine, while Article 98 also created a new state, the independent Hashemite Kingdom of Hejaz. The independent kingdom was short-lived and was eventually folded into modern Saudi Arabia following its conquest by the family Saud in 1925. The first king of Hejaz was none other than Hussein ibn Ali, who had entered into the McMahon-Hussein exchange of letters promising Arab independence in exchange for wartime cooperation against the Ottomans.

While it would of course later become a point of acerbic dispute whether the correspondence also promised Palestine to the Arabs, the fact that Hussein was a signatory to the Treaty of Sevres which expressly granted Palestine to the Jews further showed that he had no expectation that Palestine would become an Arab state.

The Treaty of Sevres was superseded by the Treaty of Lausanne in 1923, which stripped some of the harsher territorial impositions on Turkey made at Sevres, but crucially Lausanne did not revisit the question of Palestine or seek to limit the rights granted to the Jews at Sevres or at San Remo. The treaty was also signed not only by the Turks but by Hussein.

Winston Churchill in Jerusalem with British High Commissioner for Palestine Herbert Samuel.

WHITE PAPER

With the Arab post-war demands now seemingly addressed, Churchill returned to the question of Palestine.

In June 1922, conscious of rising tensions among Jews and Arabs in Palestine, Churchill gave "renewed consideration to the existing political situation"[28] there. The outcome was a "White Paper", a British government report handing down recommendations and proposals. A benign term, it would take on a sinister and deathly meaning for European Jews in the coming years.

Churchill's White Paper identified that Arab grievances stemmed from "… partly exaggerated interpretations of the meaning of the [Balfour] Declaration [and] unauthorized statements to the effect that the purpose ... was to create a wholly Jewish Palestine."²⁹

Churchill sought to quash these suggestions, which were being used by Arab leaders to incite against the Jews.³⁰ Churchill was able to point to a resolution passed by the Zionist Congress in Carlsbad in September 1921 which expressed the "determination of the Jewish people to live with the Arab people on terms of unity and mutual respect, and together with them to make the common home into a flourishing community, the upbuilding of which may assure to each of its peoples an undisturbed national development."³¹

Churchill also dealt with Jewish anxiety that Britain would relent in the face of Arab pressure and "depart from the policy embodied in the Balfour Declaration". Such fears, wrote Churchill, were "unfounded". "The Declaration, reaffirmed ... at San Remo and again in the Treaty of Sevres, is not susceptible to change."

In the White Paper, Churchill also surveyed the land. He considered the magnitude of the Jewish achievements there in the brief time that migration had been open to them.

> During the last two or three generations the Jews have recreated in Palestine a community, now numbering 80,000, of whom about one fourth are farmers or workers upon the land. This community has its own political organs; an elected assembly for the direction of its domestic concerns; elected councils in the towns; and an organization for the control of its schools. It has its elected Chief Rabbinate and Rabbinical Council for the direction of its religious affairs. Its business is conducted in Hebrew as a vernacular language, and a Hebrew Press serves its needs. It has its distinctive intellectual life and displays considerable economic activity. This community, then, with its town and country population, its political, religious, and social organizations, its own language, its own customs, its own life, has in fact "national" characteristics.³²

When the author Mark Twain travelled to the land in 1869, he noted its ugliness. "Of all the lands there are for dismal scenery, Palestine must be the prince ... the hills are barren ... the valleys are unsightly deserts, Palestine is desolate and unlovely."[33] Churchill had observed that the Jews had converted this forgotten land into a burgeoning new proto-state, a place where commerce and ingenuity were beginning to thrive.

"To provide full opportunity for the Jewish people to display its capacities", Churchill continued, "it is essential that it should know that it is in Palestine as of right and not on the sufferance.[34]

PALESTINE PARTITIONED

Article 25 of the Mandate document had enabled Britain to "withhold application" of the Mandate to lands to the east of the Jordan River, which came to be known as "Transjordan". This in effect entitled Britain to split Palestine in two, creating one territory running between the Jordan River and the Mediterranean Sea, to which the Mandate had to be applied, and a second territory running east of the River and bordering the lands of the Arabian Peninsula, over which the Mandate (including the responsibilities to the Jews) would have no application.

In September 1922, the British presented the "Transjordan Memorandum" to the League of Nations, which did just that. It formally dissected Palestine along the Jordan River creating Transjordan in the east and confining Palestine to the wedge between the River and the Sea.

Winston Churchill, now Secretary of State for the Colonies, planned to honor the McMahon-Hussein Correspondence by granting the Arabs statehood in Transjordan and Iraq while delivering on the Balfour Declaration and subsequent treaties by granting the Jews their home in Palestine. Hussein's son, Faisal was to be appointed king of Iraq, while his younger son Abdullah would rule Transjordan. Britain recognized Transjordan as an independent government on 15 May 1923.

This dealt a major blow to the Zionists, who had anticipated a state on both sides of the Jordan, encompassing much of the Jewish ancestral lands and the entirety of the Mandate territory.

The Zionist response to the cutting apart of Palestine and reduction of its territory would cause a serious rupture in the Zionist movement itself, one that arguably persists to this day. Ze'ev Jabotinsky, who had founded the Zion Mules Corps with Trumpeldor in Alexandria, now led the revisionist camp of Zionism. These were territorial maximalists, who refused to countenance a Jewish state in anything less than the original Mandate territory, including Transjordan. They challenged the conciliatory stance of leaders like Weizmann, and demanded an unflinching, muscular brand of diplomacy that would mirror the uncompromising approach adopted by the Arabs.

Jabotinsky viewed the Jordan River not as the eastern frontier of the new Jewish homeland but as its "spine". To Jabotinsky, the exclusion of lands to the east of the Jordan from the grant to the Jews constituted a "historical and practical injustice." He argued, "historically, the East Jordan Land was always part of Jewish Palestine: the Jews settled there even before the conquest of Western Palestine."[35]

While the notion of a Jewish state on both sides of the Jordan River has passed into irrelevance, the guiding principles of Jabotinsky's revisionism remain a feature of the Israeli political landscape. Jabotinsky steadfastly believed that conceding territory in the hope of peace was a betrayal of Zionism founded on a delusion that would only bring more demands and more conflict. This is a view shared by many on the political right in today's Israel.

By the end of 1923, the season of treaty-making had concluded. The defeated instigators of the Great War had paid for their actions with the loss of their empires while a movement of liberation was sweeping through Europe and the Middle East under the watch of the victorious powers. The Jews emerged with the recognition they long craved. They stood recognized as a people, with a national identity and a right to return to their former home to proclaim their state. The Balfour Declaration had been thrice inducted into international law through the San Remo Resolution, the Treaties of Sevres and Lausanne, and the League of Nations Mandate for Palestine.

As Chaim Weizmann would note in his memoirs, the effect of the Mandate was to convert the Balfour Declaration from "a policy position into an international legal obligation accepted by the international community as a whole."[36]

The enormity of attaining legal recognition for the aims of Zionism would not be lost on the Jews, a people first made a nation by Moses the lawgiver.

Meanwhile, following the Transjordan Memorandum, Palestine had been partitioned by the League of Nations. But far from satisfying Arab demands, it would localize the site of mainstream Zionist aspirations and the counter-movement intent on destroying them, to the small tract of land between the Mediterranean Sea and the River Jordan.

BALFOUR'S NOTE

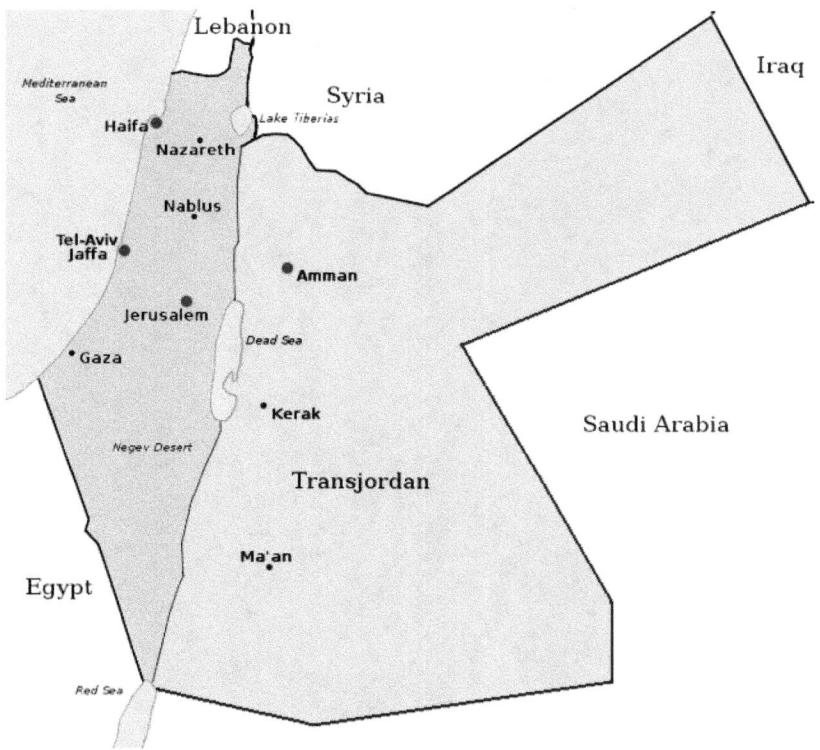

Palestine partitioned, (Creative Commons).

7

CLASH

Through the post-war treaties and the formation of the League of Nations, the international community had identified two major obstacles that had to be overcome for the restoration of Jewish self-rule to Palestine. First, a healthy Jewish presence in the land had to be achieved. Second, the Jews would have to establish the practical means by which they could govern themselves.

The first problem had been identified by Wilson at the Paris Conference when he noted that the Jews, at that time, accounted for "barely a sixth of the total population of 700,000 in Palestine."[1] A system of Jewish minority rule over a vastly non-Jewish majority would be an injustice and a recipe for perpetual conflict. Wilson observed that owing to the Jews' special circumstances, as the exiled, scattered progeny of the indigenous people of the land that had maintained an unbroken physical and cultural connection there, the Jews deserved a "privileged position" in Palestine. This meant that the Jews would be permitted to return and resettle provided they did so "without sacrificing the rights of non-Jews."[2]

The problem of Jewish minority status in the land was expressly addressed in the Mandate, which placed a positive obligation on the British to "facilitate Jewish immigration under suitable conditions and [to] encourage ... close settlement by Jews, on the land, including State lands and waste lands not required for public purposes (Article 6)."[3]

The second problem, the transition to self-government, had been addressed by the international community upon the formation of the League of Nations, where it was determined that the emancipated Ottoman lands would be overseen by a great power (Britain in the case of Palestine), which would act as "trustee" until such time as the native peoples were "able to stand alone."[4]

The Jews took to the second task, of ensuring they were able to "stand alone", with admirable self-reliance, seizing the chance to rebuild their homeland and finally organize a society according to their traditions and visions for the future.

In the early years of the British Mandate, the practical fulfilment of Zionism was being achieved at a cracking pace. Between 1924 and 1927, 65,000 Polish Jews settled in Palestine.[5] Tel Aviv, founded by the building society on the dunes outside Jaffa, was flourishing. The independent institutions that were required for effective Jewish self-government were arising and being ever refined and developed – organized labor, defense, higher education. The Hebrew University, the setting of the cornerstone of which was heralded as a great achievement by Woodrow Wilson in 1918, was rapidly evolving into a crucial institution that would attract Jewish scholars and ambitious students – the very best and brightest – from throughout the world. Sigmund Freud, Albert Einstein, Martin Buber, Weizmann, and more than a dozen Nobel laureates would in time all pass through the university as students, teachers or governors.

Having secured their legal rights to the land and with the rapid development of the institutions of statehood, the establishment of a Jewish homeland in a matter of years seemed a formality.

However, the success of the Jews in cultivating the land, in building an economy and moving towards autonomy created an inevitable sense of alienation and disenfranchisement among the non-Jewish majority. Viewed through the prism of post-war reconstruction and the competing claims to the lands liberated from Ottoman colonial rule, the Arabs had done considerably well. They had succeeded in achieving the partition of Palestine and the creation of a Palestinian-Arab state on the east bank of the Jordan River, dashing Jewish hopes of a state in all of the territory that had originally been designated by the Allied powers as Palestine. The Arabs had also been granted a pathway to self-rule in Syria, Lebanon, Iraq, the Arabian Peninsula and Yemen.

But treaties concluded in Europe and the outcomes of Jewish and Arab political maneuvering in Paris little affected the Arabs living in the remaining part of Palestine between the Jordan River and the Mediterranean Sea.

Their roots in Palestine were often deep also, whether they had arrived in Palestine from other parts of the Middle East, or had lived there for generations and knew no other home. The idea of being governed by Jews, a people whose status in Islamic lands had always been one of inferiority, was abhorrent to them. It mattered little that the Zionists had spoken in explicit terms about peaceful co-existence, or that the rights granted to the Jews from the Balfour Declaration onwards expressly protected the non-Jewish inhabitants. Even the vastly improving systems of agriculture, industry and sanitation, increases in arable lands, new centers of culture and education, all made possible by Jewish investment and endeavor, could not dispel the feeling that a land the Arabs held to be theirs was slipping from their grasp. This mix of rapidly shifting economic and political conditions coupled with feelings of racial and religious superiority, created a perfect environment for an outpouring of popular outrage.

The Islamic festival of Nebi Musa, had long been marked by a peaceful procession of much revelry and color, which would pass through the streets of Jerusalem to a site near Jericho, which Muslims believe to be the burial place of Moses. In 1920, the gathering descended into violence. Chants of "All of Palestine is ours and the Jews are our dogs," could be heard as Jewish shops in Jerusalem were looted, five Jews were killed and more than 200 Jews were injured.[6]

The incident laid bare the simmering tensions, the fusion of religious fervor with rising Arab nationalism, which the diligent treaty-making in Europe and post-war reconstruction could hardly address.

Among the procession that day was a twenty-five year old Arab Jerusalemite who held a lowly post in the British military administration in Damascus. He was the stepbrother of the leader of the procession and the scion of a prominent family that claimed descent from the prophet Mohammed. Some accounts of the Nebi Musa riot held the young man to have been the chief instigator of the violence, others maintain he was merely an inspired observer. The British seemed to take the former view and sentenced him to ten years' imprisonment for his hand in the violence; a sentence he would avoid by fleeing to Damascus before being granted a pardon by the British High Commissioner for Palestine, Herbert

Samuel. This enabled him to return to Jerusalem as something of a hero to the local Arabs.

Whatever the man's precise role in the Nebi Musa disturbance of 1920, the event marked a critical moment in the burgeoning conflict between Jews and Arabs in the land. Arab leaders stoking fears of impending loss to Jewish greed and ambition, the rousing of the masses to violence in order to achieve the political aims of leaders, would remain central features of regional affairs for the bloody decades to come.

Nebi Musa also marked a decisive point in the crystallization of a distinct Arab Palestinian identity, as a direct countermovement to Zionism. Perhaps most significantly of all, it saw the ascent of that young man in the procession, Muhammad Amin al-Husseini, later Haj Amin al-Husseini, whose impact on the course of Zionism and Jewish history would be savagely profound.

The Nebi Musa procession through Jerusalem in 1920 culminated in violent anti-Jewish rioting.

HEBRON

August 1929 saw the eruption of further violence in Jerusalem as well as in Tsfat and Hebron. For the most part the manner in which it was incited and inflicted was typical of mob violence directed at minority Jewish communities throughout history.

The immediate triggers for the violence were contrived Muslim concerns about an attempt by the Jews to change the "status quo" pertaining to the Western Wall and the Temple Mount/Haram al-Sharif in Jerusalem.

The Western Wall was the last remnant of the Second Temple built on the site of the original Jewish Temple conceived by David and constructed during the reign of his son, King Solomon. It is all that remained of the outer structure of the compound after it was razed by the Romans in the year 70 CE. It was where Jerome had observed Jewish peasants gathering in the 4th century CE, weeping and lamenting their subjugation and loss. And it was where the Jews held regular prayers from at least the 16th century.

The alleged transgression of the Jews was to first place a temporary partition to separate male and female worshippers during prayers, known as a *Mechitza* at the foot of the Wall, and to then attempt to place benches and chairs in the prayer area to ease the weariness of worshippers roasting in the hilltop sun.

The propositions that the Jews had forgotten their lowly place and were plotting something nefarious through their stealth and cunning, were familiar both to the victims and the perpetrators. These themes had been employed consistently both in Arab lands and in Europe to justify the release of the basest human urges upon Jewish neighbors.

In what could have easily been testimony from the York riots of 1190, a British policeman in Hebron wrote of the violence there: "Many of the townspeople were in debt to Jewish merchants, which had long been subject of resentment, so they now wreaked vengeance upon property."[7]

The violence began in Jerusalem and rapidly spread to Tsfat and to Hebron, where it was most lethal. On 16 August 1929, at the conclusion of Muslim Friday prayers, worshippers emerged to burn Jewish prayer books by the Western Wall along with the notes of petition to the Almighty ceremonially placed by Jews in the crevices of the Wall.[8]

French diplomats observed how "Arab rioters driven to a frenzy by Friday sermons stabbed to death Jewish passers-by who had the misfortune to cross their path …"[9] Foreign witnesses saw "… women with their breasts cut, unfortunates burned alive, further cases of throats cut, eyes gouged etc."[10] A child survivor of the violence in Hebron, Shlomo Slonim, then a boy of one, suffered a stab wound to the head and had fingers on his right hand partially severed.[11] Twenty-two Jews barricaded in the Slonim home were murdered by Arab rioters.

The "Western Wall Riots" of August 1929, marked a defining moment in the history of Jewish-Arab relations in Palestine and established the rhythm of the anti-Zionist campaign. The rioting was based on a macabre logic that if diplomacy and political maneuvering failed to achieve the objectives of the Arabs, violence could be used to test the staying power of both the Jews and the British. After Hebron, the tactical use of violence to seek policy change or achieve political transformation became a reliable instrument for the Arab leadership.

The political outcomes from the Hebron violence were near immediate. The British, determined to maintain the peace and avoid a costly entanglement, decided to limit further Jewish migration to placate the Arabs. This would violate the terms of the Mandate and deal a direct blow to the project of achieving Jewish self-government. Nevertheless, the British sought to justify the policy on the basis that Jewish migration had to be curtailed so as not to exceed the economic capacity of the land to absorb new arrivals. In fact, it had been largely as a result of Jewish migration and the establishment of industry and institutions by the Jews that the economic conditions had improved in Palestine. This in turn had attracted further Arab migration to Palestine, swelling the Arab population to over a million by about 1930.[12]

The Arabs now called for an end to Jewish migration, an abandonment of the pledge to establish a Jewish national home and the prohibition of land sales to Jews.[13]

Strengthening the hand of the Arabs was the fact that the British had deep interests in India, accessed via the Suez Canal in Egypt, and throughout the Middle East. The Balfour Declaration and the post-war treaties now seemed to belong to another time, and were the outgrowths of a war that was now finished. Meanwhile, the threat of cascading violence throughout the Middle East over the issue of Palestine, was a present concern, one brought to the attention of the British in the clearest terms. The President of the Arab Executive in Palestine, Musa Kazim Pasha told a senior British official that "there would be an armed uprising" unless the Jewish national home idea was discarded.[14]

Haj Amin al-Husseini, now the Grand Mufti of Jerusalem and leader of the Supreme Muslim Council, had through a combination of religious distortion and political rhetoric, skillfully framed the question of Palestine not as a local conflict but a paramount Islamic concern. In doing so, he sought to internationalize the conflict and harness the political and economic power of the Arab and Islamic world for what had become his defining purpose, the thwarting of Zionism by any means necessary.

Al-Husseini made opposition to the Jews a national and religious duty, a matter of Arab pride and Islamic doctrine. Coexistence with the Jews would now be considered a cowardly and disloyal proposition.

Under his leadership, the tale that the Jews were planning the destruction of the Al-Aqsa Mosque in Jerusalem and calls for Palestine's Muslims to defend holy places from the Jews intensified. An edition of the Jewish paper, *Davar,* published just days before the Hebron massacre, noted escalating rumors among the Muslims that Jews had cursed Islam and intended to capture their holy places.[15] A Dutch journalist wrote that "falsified photographs showing the Omar Mosque of Jerusalem in ruins, with an inscription that the edifice had been bombed by the Zionists, were handed out to the Arabs of Hebron as they were leaving their place of worship on Friday evening."[16] In the days after the massacre, a student leaflet circulated in Jerusalem declared, "O Arab! Remember that the Jew is your strongest enemy and the enemy of your ancestors since olden times. Do not be misled by his tricks, for it is he who tortured Christ and poisoned Mohammed ... Save yourself and your Fatherland from the grasp of the foreign intruder and greedy Jew."[17]

In the face of orchestrated violence in Palestine and the apprehension of further unrest throughout the Middle East, the

British Government commissioned a report which considered the causes of the violence and presented policy recommendations to avoid future outbreaks.

The Shaw Commission Report published in 1930, found that "there can, in our view, be no doubt that racial animosity on the part of the Arabs, consequent upon the disappointment of their national political aspirations and fear for their economic future, was the fundamental cause of the outbreak."[18]

Perhaps underestimating the extent of the "racial animosity", the Commission recommended a series of measures, including political gestures and economic incentives, that it believed would satisfy the local Arabs and dissuade them from further violence. Chief among these was the regulation of "excessive immigration" by Jews and a promise to consult with the Arabs with regard to future Jewish migration. This effectively placed control over a key requirement to the fulfilment of Zionism, in the hands of implacable anti-Zionists.

The British then delivered a further White Paper, which set out its new policy in Palestine in light of the 1929 bloodshed. It is a document that starkly reveals the extent of the British predicament. The instruments of international law from the Balfour Declaration to the San Remo Conference and the League of Nations Mandate for Palestine all sought to delicately balance the realization of a Jewish national home in Palestine with the aspirations of non-Jewish peoples in the land. But how could the British both deliver to the Jews what they had promised and satisfy the Arabs when the central demand of the Arabs was the denial of a Jewish state?

The White Paper delivered a rebuke to both sides, but ultimately settled on a path of appeasement of the Arabs. Now, rather than seeking to fulfill their obligations under the Mandate, the British would make land purchases by Jews and Jewish migration to Palestine subject to Arab acquiescence.

Chaim Weizmann was dismayed by the White Paper and resigned as President of the Zionist Organization and Jewish Agency following its release. But he did not cease his advocacy, marshalling his peerless capacity for logic and persuasion, he compelled the British to reconsider their position on Jewish migration. He spoke of the increasingly dire, suffocating state imposed on world Jewry, unwanted in Europe and with doors closed to them in the Americas and elsewhere. All that remained for the Jews was Palestine and now the White Paper threatened that too.

The Jews, Weizmann beseeched, had carried with them "... a stubborn, stiff-necked attachment to a country which many of us have not seen, but which has been the central part of our history, which has made us look upon Palestine as the country where we wanted to find the realization of an age old dream."[19]

Weizmann was able to prevail upon the British that it would be unjust to now bar the Jews from the land that had been promised to them. This prompted the British to revise its policy on Jewish migration and land purchases.

But the violence of 1929 had nevertheless resulted in a major political victory for the Arabs. They had tested how steadfast the British would remain to their international obligations and promises to the Jews and had found them wanting. The events of 1929 had also established Haj Amin Al-Husseini as an astute leader who could stand up to both the Jews and the British, and win.

The violence in Hebron and beyond also impacted on the psyche of the Jews of Palestine. Just as the poet Bialik had surveyed the carnage of the Kishinev pogrom and what it had done to the entire Jewish nation, another Jewish writer, S.Y. Agnon sought to make sense of the 1929 massacres.

Capturing the despair and betrayal felt by the Jews of Palestine, brutalized by their Arab neighbors just as they had been in Europe, Agnon wrote: "now my attitude is this. I do not hate them and I do not love them; I do not wish to see their faces. In my humble opinion, we shall now build a large ghetto of half a million Jews in Palestine, because if we do not, we will, heaven forbid, be lost."[20]

A SECOND PARTITION

It had been folly to attempt to navigate a middle path between Zionism on the one hand, and a violent opposition to Zionism on the other. This was becoming apparent to the British themselves as the violence of 1929 and the ensuing policy realignments did nothing to cool tensions or to foster harmony between the Jews and Arabs in Palestine. An Arab revolt against the British had broken out in 1936 and Al-Husseini had called a general strike.

Now two decades after Balfour, the British were looking for a durable solution to end their Palestinian entanglement while remaining honorable to their promises to the peoples of the land.

The outcome was the Peel Commission of 1937, a British Royal Commission charged with proposing a plan for resolution of the Jewish-Arab conflict in Palestine. Presented to the British Cabinet on 25 June 1937, the Peel Commission Report called for the partition of Palestine, and the creation of a Jewish state on just four per cent of the original area of the Mandate, alongside an expanded Arab Palestinian state which would merge Transjordan (previously Eastern Palestine) with most of the remaining land of Palestine to create a single, vast Arab state on both banks of the River Jordan.

The Report concluded, "half a loaf is better than no bread," and noted that while "partition means that neither will get what it wants ... both parties will come to realize that the drawbacks of partition are outweighed by its advantages."

After summarizing the advantages of partition to the Arabs, including alleviating their fear of being "swamped" by the Jews; national independence for the Arabs of Palestine; along with financial incentives; the Report then presented the benefits to the Jews:

> (a) Partition secures the establishment of the Jewish National Home and relieves it from the possibility of its being subjected in the future to Arab rule.
>
> (b) Partition enables the Jews in the fullest sense to call their National Home their own: for it converts it into a Jewish State. Its citizens will be able to admit as many Jews into it as they themselves believe can be absorbed.

The Commission argued that partition, even this half loaf that would exclude the holiest Jewish cities of Jerusalem and Hebron, "will attain the primary objective of Zionism – a Jewish nation, planted in Palestine, giving its nationals the same status in the world as other nations give theirs. They will cease at last to live a minority life."[21]

In many ways, the Peel Commission was a disaster for the Jews, a further capitulation to Arab violence, and the product of waning idealism and increasing fatigue in Britain's international outlook. Palestine had already been partitioned and a wholly Arab Palestinian state had been created on the east bank of the

Jordan River. The 1930 White Paper had credited the Jews with establishing its own "political organs; an elected assembly for the direction of its domestic concerns; elected councils in the towns; an organization for the control of its schools." By the time of the Peel Commission, the Jewish population of Palestine was over 400,000, now a third of the total population. The Jews felt that they had fulfilled their part of the bargain, in settling and cultivating the land and were ready for statehood. The confinement of the Jews to now merely seventeen percent of the land between the Mediterranean Sea and the River Jordan seemed a compromise too far.

David Ben-Gurion, the leader of the Jews in Palestine, spoke of aspects of the partition plan as a "… great blessing for the Arab State – and for us it is a question of life, existence, protection of culture … freedom and independence."[22]

With flames lapping at the door of European Jewry, and the one million Jews of the Middle East fearing what would come from their Arab neighbors as the conflict in Palestine became more intense, Ben-Gurion saw the need to sever a limb to save the body. At the Twentieth Zionist Congress in Zurich in August 1937, the Jewish leadership, including Weizmann reluctantly acceded to the idea of partition and subsequently began to formulate proposals for territorial adjustments. But this became of no consequence. The Arabs rejected the proposal outright.

Al-Husseini had given evidence, in rather contemptuous terms, to the Peel Commission, in which he not only rejected absolutely the idea of a Jewish state in any borders or of any size, but of even living alongside the Jews in a majority Arab state.

In September 1937, in Bludan, Syria, an Arab congress of over 400 delegates met to reject the partition of Palestine, declaring instead that its goal was "liberation of the country and establishment of an Arab government."[23] Transjordan's King Abdullah stood apart as a lone Arab voice in favor of partition, foreseeing a looming catastrophe, and a failure of Arab Palestinian leadership, through which Palestine would pass into Jewish hands.

The Peel Commission Report was never implemented. It stands as the first Arab rejection of a two-state solution in favor of the pursuit of the total denial of Jewish self-rule.

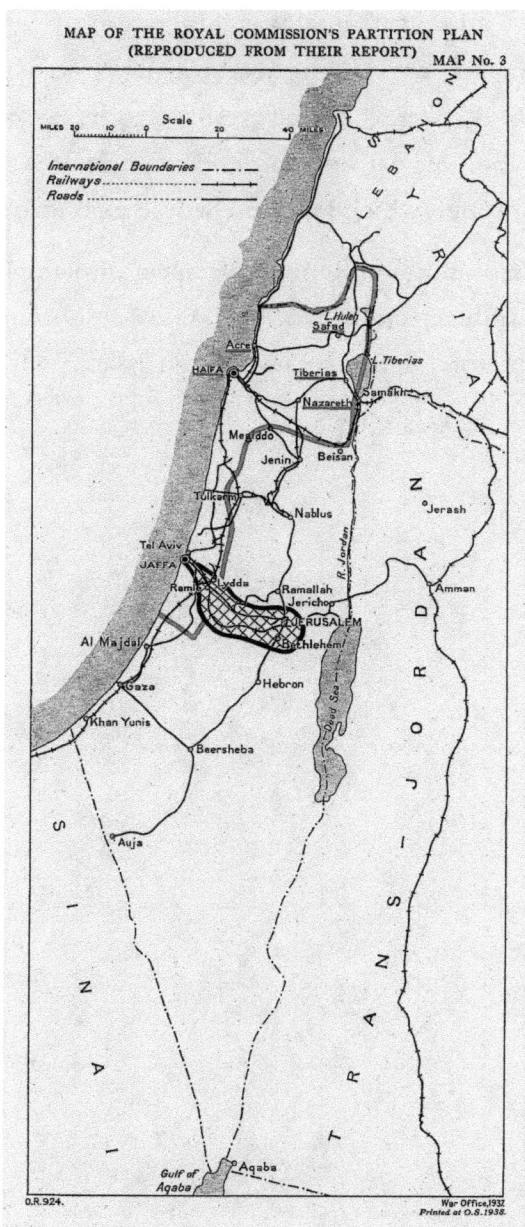

The proposed partition of the Mandate territory to create a Jewish state and an Arab state in Palestine, as recommended by the Peel Commission of 1937. The proposed Jewish State on 4% of the original Mandate territory is shown in thick black line. The cross-hatched area represents the proposed international zone.

A NEW WHITE PAPER

Two years later, as the Arab revolt and violent attacks on Jews in Palestine escalated and were being met with reprisals by Jewish militias, the British released a final White Paper.

With the rejection of the Peel Plan by the Arabs and no end in sight to the violence, the 1939 White Paper called the idea of partition "impracticable", and called for the establishment, within 10 years, of an independent "Palestine State", in which Jews and Arabs would "share authority in government ..."[24]

Citing "lamentable disturbances of the past three years [caused by] intense Arab apprehension ..." of further Jewish migration, and noting the failed hope that "... in time the Arab population would recognize the advantages to be derived from Jewish settlement and development in Palestine ..."[25] the Paper called for the imposition of a migrant quota. Over a period of 5 years, no more than 75,000 Jews were to enter Palestine.

If the Peel Commission proposal promised to "attain the primary objective of Zionism", being a Jewish state in some part of the Jewish ancestral lands, the White Paper of 1939 made the fulfilment of Zionism a practical impossibility. Jews would forever remain a minority in the land and the notion of a Jewish state in Palestine had been replaced with Jewish minority status in Palestine.

Despite eventually accepting the Peel Commission's partition plan, Weizmann initially said of it: "Could there be a more appalling fraud of the hopes of a martyred people than to reduce it to a ghetto status in the very land where it was promised national freedom."[26]

How truer still were Weizmann's words when applied to the White Paper which was to extinguish any prospect of a Jewish national home and merely shift the minority life of the Jews from Europe and the Islamic world, to Palestine.

The Jewish Agency called the White Paper a "surrender to Arab terrorism" and blasted feckless British policy in a public statement:

> It is in the darkest hour of Jewish history that the British Government proposes to deprive the Jews of their last hope and to close the road back to their Homeland. It is a cruel blow, doubly cruel because it comes from the government of a great nation which has extended a helping hand to the Jews, and whose position must rest on foundations of moral authority and international good faith. This blow will not subdue the Jewish people. The historic bond between the people and the land of Israel cannot be broken. The Jews will never accept the closing to them of the gates of Palestine nor let their national home be converted into a ghetto. The Jewish pioneers who, during the past three generations, have shown their strength in the unbuilding of a derelict country, will from now on display the same strength in defending Jewish immigration, the Jewish home and Jewish freedom.[27]

With war looming in Europe, the White Paper was intended to finally satisfy the Arabs of Palestine and win over the wider Arab world. Britain's experience in the Great War was that the Arabs could either be thorny opponents or useful allies if a European war should metastasize into Asia.

For all their earlier diplomatic achievements, on this occasion, the Zionist leadership had been badly outmaneuvered and were taught a harsh lesson on Middle East strategy. The Jews had sought to be the more reasonable party, adopting their usual conciliatory posture in the hope that this would bring them in alignment with the British arbiters. But when dealing with a declining imperial power, stretched in all directions, wearied by Palestine and no longer romantically attached to the idea of Jewish national return, the Jewish willingness to compromise was taken for weakness and ruthlessly exploited.

At a conference of Jewish and Arab leaders convened by the British prior to the adoption of the White Paper, the Arabs and the British presented a joint position calling for significant restrictions on further Jewish migration to Palestine. This position was repugnant to the Jewish side, both for its incompatibility with the fulfilment of Zionism and because it would slam the door on the increasingly desperate European Jews. Yet Weizmann struck an accommodating tone, agreeing in principle to the "slow down" of migration and even mentioning a possible quota of "50-60,000 to enter Palestine each year."[28] This floored the rest of the Jewish delegation, which apparently had no fore-warning that Weizmann would make such a statement.

Perhaps Weizmann had intended to establish his reasonableness and would have later diluted or walked-back his offer. Perhaps he had been seduced by the words of praise uttered by the Arab side for the Jewish development of Palestine, which Weizmann had noted with pleasure and then responded to with his own words of grace and gratitude. Or perhaps Weizmann was wary of the weakness of his bargaining position and didn't wish to overplay his hand.

Regardless, this had been a misstep by Weizmann, one that showed that just as the Jews had come around to the idea of partition and the tiny statelet offered by the Peel Commission, the Jews would surely take whatever was being offered here too. The Arabs on the other hand, had maintained a consistent position of outright rejection of Jewish migration, Jewish land acquisition and a Jewish state, all backed by the threat of violence. This concerned the British most of all at a time when war with Germany loomed large following Hitler's dismemberment of Czechoslovakia in the previous year.

The White Paper was adopted despite Jewish anguish and Arab demands that its severe restrictions on Jewish migration in fact be extended to a total prohibition. Britain's Prime Minister Neville Chamberlain told his Cabinet, "we are now compelled to consider the Palestine problem mainly from the point of view of its effect on the international situation ... if we must offend one side, let us offend the Jews rather than the Arabs."[29]

British appeasement was not confined to its early dealings with Nazi Germany. In the hope of satisfying the Arabs, the British had jettisoned their obligations under law, repudiated their commitment to the Jews, and had foreclosed on the idea of a Jewish national home in any part of the ancient Jewish homeland.

This was made all the more callous by the growing severity of the Jewish plight in Europe. The world had witnessed the *Kristallnacht* pogroms across Germany in November 1938, and seen the Jews gradually expunged from public life in Germany through the Nuremburg Laws. Now the German advance eastward placed millions of Jews in Poland and the Soviet Union within the clutches of a regime whose defining ideology was antisemitism. In adopting the White Paper, Britain had all but sealed the Jews in a Europe that was poised to obliterate them.

8

INFERNO

The Holocaust, the name given to the 20th century genocide of the European Jews, is often examined in isolation. Something without precedent and without successor. Indeed, the enormity of the killing, the unsparing barbarity and cool sophistication with which it was carried out; its genesis in the center of enlightened Western Europe, all contribute to the uniqueness of the event. This in turn means that it is largely viewed as an aberrant thing, a deviation in the progression of human history.

In reality, the events of the Holocaust were entirely predictable and had been shown to the Jews in preview over and over again.

The expulsion of the Jews from Spain and England showed how dispensable this ancient nation was. The slaughter of Jews in York and Odessa showed how easily a mob could be compelled to kill men, women and children in a great release of pent up frustration in times of political upheaval or economic downturn. The lowered rifles of the police in Kishinev showed that at best police units would stand aside for the mob, at worst they would be the mob. Bogdan Chmelnitsky had demonstrated the sadism, vulgarity and blood revelry that abounded in seemingly ordinary men. The Dreyfus Affair had shown that the mob cared nothing for good citizenry or a record of civic participation. The Granada massacre had shown that having access to high places, petitioning courtiers and rulers, was meaningless once the tide had turned.

How fickle are the rules and norms we establish, the order we think we have, the customs we expect to be followed, in the face of overwhelming evil backed by unstoppable force.

The Jews carried with them every story of woe, absorbed every outrage and betrayal into their collective consciousness, had developed a tradition of storytelling, parent to child, and boasted a liturgy overflowing with examples of what could, and frequently did, happen to them. Leon Pinsker warned that the Jews were viewed as "nothing but vagrants and parasites, without the protection of the law."[1] Jewish scripture warned that their Lord could abandon the Jews and "let loose the wild beasts against you, which shall bereave you of your children and make you few in number."[2] But the horrors of the past were not taken as harbingers of worse to come but of evidence that no matter how dire the outlook, this too would surely pass. But this did not pass. Despite all the warnings, the Jews of Europe continued to live in a state of perfect self-delusion, on the precipice of a complete inferno.

Before the killing could begin, the Nazis had to overcome enormous practical challenges such as defining who is a Jew, determining the treatment of the offspring of mixed-marriages, and accounting for converts to Christianity. It would be one thing to dispose of undesired rural Jewish communities in the east, they would hardly be missed. But prominent Jews, who had deep connections, often through intermarriage, into the wider community would have to be treated more delicately. Then there was the issue of international reaction, quelling the outrage that would surely come from such persecution and human rights abuses. And the process of identifying Jews would be an enormous challenge. The Jews have a propensity for community organizing and scrupulous bookkeeping, which would make it easier to identify and locate Jews who maintained ties to their community. But what of the Jews whose affiliation with the community had long lapsed? What of the newly conquered territories of which the Germans had no knowledge? These problems all had to be solved before the Germans could even consider how they would carry out the process of ghettoization, deportation and extermination itself, which would require enormous human and financial resources to be diverted from a global military campaign.

In the end, the Germans overcame each challenge with an almost impressive diligence and enterprise. They also demonstrated a truly extraordinary understanding of human nature, and specifically of the nature of the Jew. The Nazis posited that the level of hatred of the Jews was such that they could be systematically stripped of all rights, removed from the wider population, robbed blind, and eventually murdered with little or no outcry or resistance. They correctly evaluated that the international reaction would be trivial, particularly when such outrages were taking place under the cover of world war.

And they understood, perfectly, as the Zionists had, that centuries of intimidation, harassment, expulsion, humiliation and wanton slaughter had for the most part given the Jews a distinctly vulnerable character. These were not the zealots who had staved off the forces of Ancient Greece or had held out against the Romans in the fortress of Masada until the bitter end.

Instead, as the Holocaust historian, Raul Hilberg observed, the Jews of Europe had honed a distinct, formulaic reaction to danger. Their means of resistance was no longer taking to the Judean hills and launching rearguard actions. It meant petitioning governments, exploring legal measures, mounting intellectual arguments to sway public opinion. If this failed the Jews would then seek to alleviate or minimize their suffering, to evade the measures directed against them. Finally if all the preceding steps had failed, they would enter a state of helpless, hopeless paralysis which led to complete compliance.[3]

Throughout the Holocaust, the executioners stood incredulous at the sight of Jews digging their own graves, at Jewish community leaders dutifully depositing lists of Jewish births and deaths to Nazi bureaucrats, and mothers imploring their daughters to offer their bodies to SS men in the futile, misguided hope that this will ameliorate their suffering, save others or save themselves.

At the same time, we have to understand that in most cases the Jews had no idea of the fate that awaited them and were completely taken in by the elaborate deceptions of the Nazis who promised them resettlement, work and food. Communications were poor. Rumors abounded of Nazi killing squads hunting Jews, of deportations to "the East" from which no one would return. But these accounts seemed too far-fetched to be believed.

In any event, the practical capacity of the Jews to resist was virtually non-existent. Throughout Europe, the Jews had come to rely on the goodwill of their neighbors and the functioning of laws and societal structures to protect them. They had no real means of self-defense and were outgunned and outnumbered in every conceivable way. They were certainly incapable of defending themselves against an unimaginably vast and comprehensive apparatus of death consisting of state power, military force, and supplemented by local populations and police units who willfully collaborated with the Nazis in virtually every place they entered.

The problem of persuading civilized societies to actively aid in the genocide or at least remain passive, was readily overcome also. For this, the Germans had their antisemitic predecessors to thank. The Roman Empire, the Church and its marauding Crusaders, nationalist figures like Chmelnytsky and Petyluria, intellectual titans like Martin Luther, had long established that Jewish blood was cheap, and had imprinted on the collective psyche a distinct characterization of the Jewish people.

The Secret Protocols of the Elders of Zion was a fabricated document purporting to be the minutes ('protocols') of a meeting of Jewish elders plotting strategies for Jewish global domination. It was produced by the Russian secret service at the beginning of the 20th century to try to deflect popular anti-government sentiment away from the Tsar and instead direct the fury of the masses on a weak and familiar foe.

It was readily absorbed into the public imagination. Complete with tales of nocturnal meetings in the forests of Europe, the themes of the publication – the cunning, the deception, the scheming, the controlling, the arrogant manipulation of the lives of good, ordinary folk, all sat wholly within the longstanding depiction of who the Jew was and how he behaved. Its mass publication through the largesse of American industrialist, Henry Ford, allowed the Protocols to reach a near-global audience. Pinning every subsequent economic calamity, revolution or epidemic on the Jews became easier still.

It was not until 1921 that articles in *The Times of London* revealed that large tracts of the Protocols had been plagiarized from an 1864 work of French political satire (Maurice Joly's *Dialogue aux enfers entre Machiavel et Montesquieu*), which had attacked the regime of Napoleon III, and had absolutely nothing to do with the Jews.[4] In 1935, the Protocols was proved to be a fabrication in a court case in Bern, Switzerland. Judge Walter Meyer, a Christian who had not heard of the Protocols earlier, said in his judgment, "I hope, the time will come when nobody will be able to understand how in 1935 nearly a dozen sane and responsible men were able for two weeks to mock the intellect of the Bern court discussing the authenticity of the so-called Protocols, the very Protocols that, harmful as they have been and will be, are nothing but laughable nonsense."[5] This "laughable nonsense" artfully designed to dupe the foolish and the prejudiced, remains in print to this day.

Full of paradoxes, unsupported by fact or reason, the depiction of the Jew satisfied the human urge to see and understand evil and to find a cause for life's horrors and misfortunes. The Jew was cunning yet parasitic, ritualistically clean but plainly filthy, lazy yet all-powerful, repelled by the Gentile yet desirous of their women, studious yet utterly perverse. And always, inferior and most importantly, unchangeable.

Critically, in order to allow otherwise decent and moral people to descend into such a depth of loathing for their fellow man, it had been necessary to not only completely dehumanize the Jew, to reduce him to the status of a flea, but also to frame any action against him a helpless resort to self-defense against a nation of deviants and murderers.

Luther had called the Jews "thirsty bloodhounds and murderers of all Christendom" … and claimed that they had "poisoned water and wells, stolen children, and torn and hacked them apart". "Christians have been tortured and persecuted by the Jews all over the world," he said.[6]

In 1895, decades before the world had even heard of Hitler, the speaker of the German parliament called the Jews "cholera germs".[7]

And what is left to be done with such a thing but to destroy it? As the Holocaust historian Yehuda Bauer noted, "one does not argue with parasites".[8]

DESTRUCTION

As it happened, the process of removing the Jews from the societies of which they formed an integral part was unproblematic. As the specter of war loomed and eventually set in, the fact that the Jews of Europe were literally disappearing was of very little concern. Their vast personal and communal possessions were harvested, they were confined physically to ghettoes where they were forced to live as the insular, diseased wretched race that propaganda had said they were all along, and from there they were eventually taken to be killed – men, women, children.

From September 1939, within days of the commencement of

the war with the invasion of Poland, shootings of Jewish civilians in Nazi-occupied areas began. The process of mass extermination commenced in June 1941 after the Nazi invasion of the Soviet Union. The initial method of killing was through mobile killing squads, known as Einsatzgruppen, that moved on the heels of the advancing German army. Their mission was to comb the cities and towns for Jews. The Einsatzgruppen units were generally made up of seasoned German soldiers, educated men in their early 30s, taken from the ranks of the SS, German Police and the Waffen-SS and supplemented by local police and volunteers. The mobility of the units and the general autonomy with which they were allowed to carry out their work was the key to their deathly effectiveness. They would move with devastating speed, trapping the large Jewish population centers before the victims could discover their fate, then returning to conduct further sweeps, sometimes days later, sometimes weeks later, in order to ensnare any Jews who had evaded the initial dragnet.

The massacre of 33,771 Jews in Kiev, carried out over two days in September 1941 in the Babi Yar ravine on the northern edge of the city, was one of the earliest mass-shootings of Jews. It was indicative of both the method of killing and the process of locating and rounding-up Jews that was perfected throughout the vast, sprawling lands of the Soviet Union.

On the morning of September 28, notices were plastered around Kiev in the German, Ukrainian and Russian languages, ordering the city's Jews (referred to in the notices by the pejorative "Yids") to assemble at a designated entry point to Babi Yar by 8am the following morning. The notices instructed the Jews to bring their "documents, money, valuables, warm clothes, underwear etc," thereby lulling the victims into believing that resettlement, and not the machine-gun, awaited them.

Anatoli Kuznetsov, a non-Jewish resident of Kiev, was twelve years old at the time of the massacre. He recalled that the Jews "started arriving while it was still dark, to be in good time to get seats in the train." Curious Ukrainians gathered on the streets to watch the wretched procession of "howling children, their old and sick, some of them weeping... with their bundles roughly tied together with string and worn-out cases made from plywood..." The reactions of the Ukrainians varied. Some expressed pity and regret, others sheltered neighbors, some acted wickedly. Indifference dominated.

Worst of all, were the instances of locals informing on hiding Jews. A German report noted that their soldiers received more tip-offs about the locations of Jews than they were able to process.

Kuznetsov would later record his observations in a memoir, titled *Babi Yar: A Document in the Form of a Novel*,[9] which also incorporated the extraordinary testimony of one of the few survivors of the massacre, Dina Pronicheva, who would relate her experience directly to Kuznetsov, and also gave evidence in the war crimes trial held in the city in 1946.

Pronicheva was a Ukrainian-Jewish actress in the Kiev Puppet Theatre. She had escorted her elderly parents to the assembly point expecting that she herself would avoid deportation by virtue of being married to an ethnic Russian. She was betrayed by her identity papers which revealed her nationality to be "Jewish", and only survived by jumping into the ravine a moment before the firing began and sheltering under piles of bodies before making her escape at nightfall. She described the moment she leapt into the abyss as like jumping into a "bath full of blood." Pronicheva was later given up to the Germans by a Ukrainian family and escaped death a second time by jumping from a moving truck that was transporting the last Jews of Kiev to the execution site.

Her testimony reveals a revelry and euphoria among German soldiers and Ukrainian auxiliaries, which contradicts the view that the Holocaust was conducted with cold bureaucratic diligence, a perspective that gained favor from Hannah Arendt's observations of the trial of Adolf Eichmann.

Pronicheva saw young Jewish women being violated by groups of German soldiers before being bayoneted to death where they lay. On occasion, a mother unable to control a hysterical child would have the child snatched away by an impatient German soldier who would proceed to dash the child's skull against a wall before handing it back to the mother. In other instances, Pronicheva recalled, soldiers would simply toss distraught babies over the wall at the assembly point "like pieces of wood".

At Babi Yar, the victims were divided into small groups, they deposited their possessions, stripped naked in the Autumn chill, before proceeding to the edge of the ravine. Local police and Ukrainian auxiliaries brought in from Western Ukraine manned the external checkpoints and saw to it that the Jews were relieved of their clothes and personal effects. The German soldiers dealt with the victims at the point of death.

Now naked, the victims were made to pass through a tight cordon of soldiers with dogs where they were clubbed mercilessly before reaching the other side. Pronicheva describes the soldiers as "drunk with fury in a sort of sadistic rage."

Naked, wounded, bewildered, the victims were powerless to resist and were obedient without recorded exception. Teetering on the edge of the ravine, they awaited the fire of machine-guns and toppled into the void beneath them. Some were not lethally wounded and bled to death under a mass of bodies. Others slowly suffocated under the earth that was heaped onto the victims at the end of each day of killing. Residents heard the "ta-ta-ta, ta-ta…" of machine-gun fire from dawn until nightfall and reported that the killing site shifted and groaned for days after the massacre. At the end of each day, soldiers descended into the ravine to club any survivors to death or to empty the pockets of those who had been killed with their clothes still on. At night, the soldiers lit bonfires, slurped coffee from aluminum cups, and helped themselves to any women designated for shooting the following day.

Babi Yar astounds for the dizzying speed with which tens of thousands of people were taken from an ordinary suburban existence to a mass expanse of concentrated death. In Kiev, it had been unnecessary to persuade the people of the city of the correctness of killing their Jews. There was no gradual separation or withdrawal of Jews from public life. When the Germans entered the city, the Jews were simply summoned and shot.

In Romania, the locals grew impatient by the orderly manner in which the Germans were developing the killing process and took matters into their own hands. In Bucharest, Jews, among them a five-year-old girl were taken to a kosher slaughterhouse, skinned alive and hung from meat hooks. In Bogdanovca, nearly 5,000 sick and infirm Jews were crammed into barns and stables which were then sprinkled with straw, doused in gasoline and set alight. The Jews of Jedbawne in Poland were similarly shut into a barn and incinerated alive by their Polish neighbors. In Budapest in late 1944, 20,000 Jews were assembled on the bank of the River Danube and shot until they toppled in.

The most common method of execution in the initial phase of the killing process was by mass shooting, usually carried out in forests or ravines. Over 1,300,000 Jews were killed in this way.[10]

The first gassing of Jews took place at the Chelmno camp in Poland. From December 1941, transportations of Jews to the camp commenced, where they were then loaded into vans which had been sealed and specially rigged so as to direct the exhaust fumes into the cabin. The victims were driven for around ten minutes by which time they died by asphyxiation and the corpses were then taken directly to pre-prepared mass graves in the adjacent Waldiager forest. By the end of the war, some 320,000 Jews had been dispatched at Chelmno.

Other death camps in Poland commenced operation after January 1942, following the formal adoption at the Wannsee Conference in Berlin of the plan to completely exterminate the Jews, in what came to be known as the "Final Solution to the Jewish Question".

The camps, Belzec, Sobibor, Treblinka, Maidanek, Auschwitz-Birkenau, were suitably positioned far enough away from metropolitan areas so that the smell of burning flesh would not bring unwanted scrutiny, but close enough to be well-served by rail lines to make human transports from all parts of occupied-Europe possible.

With the camps built and the methods of mass killing trialed and perfected, the ghettoes of Europe could be liquidated. The Jews were crammed into train wagons used for transporting cattle in which they would ride across the continent for days on end, completely without food or water, sometimes given a pause so that the corpses of loved ones could be tossed out of the wagons before continuing onward to the camps.

In some camps, the fit were put to slave labor until their bodies gave out while the very young, the old and the sick were selected for gassing immediately. The process of selection would take place on the platform immediately upon arrival. Nazi doctors looked over the human cargo, sending them to one queue or another, forever tearing sister from sister, mother from child.

The ones selected to die immediately were led into chambers which were sealed behind them before canisters of poison were released through chutes in the ceiling. When the victims ceased their writhing and their nervous systems succumbed, other inmates were charged with transferring the dead to the crematoria, clearing the chamber of visible signs of distress like bodily waste and fingernails clawed into walls, to ensure the next batch of victims would enter the chamber without disorder or resistance.

At Auschwitz, human experiments were conducted on the living, including determining the time to death from injection with various poisons, the effects of the removal of organs without anesthetic; and freezing victims to see how close they could be brought to the point of death and still be revived. If they survived the torture that masqueraded as science, their only salvation was the gas chamber.

Those who were able to survive for any length of time in the camps existed in a realm somewhere between life and death, but surely closer to death. They ate virtually nothing, slept in barns and worked outdoors in the freezing Polish winter wrapped in rags, and were rife with diseases like dysentery and typhoid from malnutrition and the absence of clean water. They could have only lived from one moment to the next in the knowledge that their families had been killed and that the same fate would strike them at any time. Such was the deathly pall about them that rats sometimes attacked the still-living, mistaking them for corpses.

In the perfect crescendo to centuries of gradually debasing and reducing the humanity of the Jewish people, they were exterminated in purpose-built camps, industrial factories of destruction, using a common pesticide, Zyklon-B.

The Nazis had honed a method of mass killing that allowed them to save their bullets for the Red Army, would spare their soldiers the potential hardship of face-to-face killing of women and children, day after day, and ensured that the Jews were made unalive at a rate of up to 15,000 people a day.[11]

Leon Pinsker had written of the ghost-like status of the Jews in exile. Herzl had said that statelessness had suspended the Jews in a lesser class to all other peoples. It was far worse than that. The Germans had skillfully tapped into everything that was hated and feared about the Jew, and reduced a proud nation that had given the world ethical monotheism, into vermin for extermination.

When the Germans were finally forced into retreat, they abandoned the camps, deploying inmates to hastily conceal the apparatus of industrial death as best they could, before killing off the remaining inmates or else sending them on long, winter death marches to other camps.

By the time the killing had ended, more than 3 million Jews had been killed in the camps. The total Jewish dead stood in the vicinity of 6 million. They died from disease in ghettos, from poison gas, mass shootings, live burial, beatings, incineration. Half of the dead were from Poland, a country in which Jewish life had accounted for some 10% of the total population. They had perished in all corners of Europe from the Baltic to France, Scandinavia to the Balkans.

Of the Jews who had lived in territories that fell to the Nazis, 78% perished. In comparison, between 1.4% to 3% of the non-Jewish population in the same territory was killed.[12] The total annihilation of the European Jews was averted only by the failure of the Germans to fully conquer the Soviet Union and to a lesser-extent Britain, the escape of some Jews from Europe before it was too late, and the liberation of the camps before the extermination work was completed.

Dynasties and entire families, great sages and common workers, Nobel laureates and humble students, babies, pensioners, whole villages and communities, had all disappeared. Thriving Jewish intellectual and cultural centers like Krakow and Vilnius that had bustled with Jewish life – seminary students, merchants, families, all manner of artisans, were now reduced to rude husks, urban memorials of human depravity.

The Jews' possessions now divvied up between the Nazi conquerors and the locals, the former inhabitants now piles of ash in the forests surrounding the camps.

How many more Freuds and Einsteins, Chagalls and Primo Levis were among them we can never know. A million Jewish children were killed. A million Anne Franks vanished in a pit of suffering.

The scholar and campaigner for prosecution of Nazi war criminals, Efraim Zuroff wrote of how the historian Shimon Dubnow was dragged from his home in the Riga ghetto to be killed. His last words to the Jews around him were, "Yidn farschreibt" – "Jews, record it all, write it all down"; while in a suburb of Kovno, Lithuania, Jews also taken to be shot scrawled a final message to any surviving brethren, "Yidn nekoma – Jews take revenge."[13]

But how could such a thing be avenged? What could be redeemed from such complete calamity?

Compounding the Jewish sense of helplessness and betrayal was the collective shrug of indifference that was the overwhelming reaction of the international community, before, during and after the slaughter. When at the request of Franklin D. Roosevelt an international conference was convened in Evian, France to discuss the question of Jewish refugees following Germany's annexation of Austria in 1938, the conference broke up with no solution to the looming crisis.

Capturing the mood of pathetic diplomatic indifference, the Australian representative, T. W. White, explained that Australia would not be taking Jewish refugees, "as we have no real racial problem, we are not desirous of importing one,"[14] as though the Nazi persecution of the Jews was really just a feud between communities.

A German observer at the conference reported to the Nazi top brass that "... a practical and concrete result that would ease the question of Jewish emigration is not possible at the moment." "The many speeches and discussions", the report told, "show that with the exception of a few countries that can still admit Jewish emigrants, there is an extensive aversion to a significant flow of emigrants either out of social considerations or out of an unexpressed racial abhorrence against Jewish emigrants."[15] Hitler was said to have drawn the conclusion from the conference that he could do with the Jews exactly as he pleased.

The following year, the MS St. Louis, a ship containing 937 Jewish refugees from Germany left Hamburg for Havana. The refugees were denied entry by Cuba, set sail for Florida where the US Coast Guard ensured they did not disembark, were further rejected by Canada, and sent back to Europe. The refugees were eventually accepted by Britain, France, Holland and Belgium after a Jewish relief agency posted a surety of $500,000.[16] Many of those accepted by countries soon to fall under Nazi occupation were eventually gassed in Auschwitz and Sobibor.

The British meanwhile, generous towards the St Louis "voyage of the damned", stood behind the 1939 Palestine White Paper with its severe restrictions on Jewish migration. Even at the conclusion of the war, the British took to sabotaging ships in foreign harbors to prevent Jewish survivors from seeking passage to Palestine.[17] In 1947, the Exodus, a ship carrying 4,500 survivors to Palestine was commandeered by the British off the coast of Haifa and returned to Europe where the refugees were forcibly removed by British soldiers and warehoused in displaced persons camps in Germany.

The killings continued even after the fall of Nazi Germany and the liberation of Europe. In Kielce, Poland in 1946, a mob, which included hundreds of mills workers, set upon Jewish Holocaust survivors, clubbing 42 to death.[18] There were reports of Jews being killed while attempting to return to their homes across Poland. In August 1945, thunderous applause greeted the passing of a resolution by the Polish Peasants Party thanking Hitler for destroying the Jews and calling for the expulsion of any survivors.[19]

The dehumanization of the Jews had been so complete that even the disaster that antisemitism had unleashed on the European continent, the bestial carnage to which millions bore witness, could not dislodge it.

The people of Europe had allowed themselves to believe that their misfortune, their poverty, their war losses, their poor crops and their national debt, were squarely the fault of the Jew. The Jewish peasants tending the land, the pious, secluded families seeking wisdom in ancient texts, the middle-class merchants of the cities, the teachers, the drunks, the scholars, the poets, the vagrants, the bankers and the children. In the final wash it just didn't matter how absurd the idea of their collective guilt was. The die had been cast over hundreds of years.

The people believed this lunacy because they wanted to believe it. And if they were wrong and they had just extinguished millions of lives for no reason at all, and war and poverty and misfortune would not go to the grave with the Jew, well at least they had blown off a little steam and enriched themselves a little in the process.

"Selection" of Hungarian Jews on the ramp at Auschwitz-II-Birkenau in German-occupied Poland, May/June 1944 (Several sources believe the photographer to have been Ernst Hoffmann or Bernharde).

Mass shooting of Jews by an Einsatzgruppe unit (Gustav Hille, Public Domain).

Prisoners at a Nazi concentration camp (Pvt. Ralph Forney, US Army, Creative Commons).

Scratch marks on a wall of a gas chamber at Auschwitz (Creative Commons).

COLLABORATION

The scale of the killing of the European Jews could not have been achieved without local collaboration. In a few places the Germans encountered resistance to the deportation and execution of the Jews, notably in Bulgaria and Denmark. But for the most part, the Germans met a mix of utter apathy and eager participation. Local police forces were particularly adept at locating hiding Jews. They knew the hiding places better than the invading Germans.

The Croatian Ustashe, the Hungarian Arrow Cross, the Latvian Arajs Commando, and similar nationalist militias throughout Europe were responsible for rounding up and massacring Jews, often acting autonomously of German directives. In some instances, they carried out killings with such sadism and frenzy that even the Germans stood appalled.

Historian Jan Grabowski chronicled the killing of Jews in Poland by ethnic Poles, intent on "realizing their own dream of a Jew-free Poland."[20] Stepan Bandera's Organization of Ukrainian Nationalists (OUP) participated in killings of Jews in pits and forests throughout the land, often quite apart from the Nazi operations.

It is among the inglorious catalogue of Nazi collaborators, those who out of shameful obedience or perverse self-interest facilitated the near destruction of an entire people, that we again encounter the ambitious Grand Mufti of Jerusalem, Haj Amin al-Husseini.

Al-Husseini had opposed any conciliation or national or civil rights for the Jews with ferocious consistency. In this respect, he was not out of step with the majority of Arab leaders. But in his decision-making regarding the Jews, Al-Husseini operated with the same sort of pathology that animated the Nazis. He was not satisfied with the 1939 White Paper, which would prevent the Jews from ever becoming more than a minority group in Palestine. Indeed, al-Husseini had rejected it outright because it permitted even limited Jewish migration to Palestine. Al-Husseini was intent on stopping the problem at its source, Europe. So long as the Jews had any organizational capacity in Europe they could lobby and push for the gradual fulfilment of Zionism, just as they had done through the endeavors of Herzl and Weizmann, the Jewish National Fund and the Zionist Congress.

At the meeting of Arab leaders in Bludan, Syria at which the Peel Commission's partition plan was rejected by the Arab side, a tract written by al-Husseini was read to the assembly. It spoke of Islam being under attack by Jews, of a Jewish plot to "annihilate the Muslims", and drew heavily on Islamic theology to justify a policy of absolute confrontation with the Jewish enemy. "Just as the Jews were able to betray Mohammed, so they will betray the Muslims today." He cited versions of the Koran and Hadith to assert that the Jews were Islam's most bitter enemy and were trying to destroy it.[21] Al-Husseini's speeches and writing on the Jews became seminal texts of modern political Islam and were distributed to audiences of hundreds of thousands in the Middle East through Arabic-language broadcasts by Nazi Germany.[22]

In depicting his people as the victims of the Jews and compelling action against them through a mix of contrived victimhood and national-religious imperative, al-Husseini was operating in parallel to the propagandists of Nazi Germany. He would borrow from and enlarge the corpus of antisemitic theory. Killing the Jews was both an honorable religious calling and a benign act of self-defense. As total war descended, the paths of the Nazis and al-Husseini would directly intersect.

Al-Husseini entered Europe under Italian protection in October 1941 and met with the German Foreign Minister Ribbentrop in Berlin the following month. A week after that, on November 28, he met with Hitler. Al-Husseini sought an alliance between the Arabs and the Nazis, citing common enemies in the Jews, Communists and the British. He lauded Hitler's support for the Arab Palestinian cause and sought a declaration from Hitler, a sort of Nazi equivalent of the Balfour Declaration, in the words of historian Tom Segev,[23] which would declare Nazi support for the elimination of a Jewish national home and political independence for the Arabs.

A now declassified CIA file on al-Husseini describes the Grand Mufti as a man of "charm", capable of "delicate manipulation", and skilled in "exploiting Muslim hatred of "infidel rule".[24] Hitler, it seems, agreed with this assessment. Reflecting on his meeting with al-Husseini, he called him an "eminently sly fox" ... of "considered cleverness".[25]

The CIA concluded him to be too clever by half. "Deluded by his own pan-Arab convictions," the dossier states, "the Mufti made the mistake of appealing to the Arab world as if it were a single entity." Nevertheless, al-Husseini was dogged and committed in his work of uniting Islamism with Nazism and applying the "final solution to the Jewish question" to Palestine.

Hitler assured him that once Europe had been dealt with and

his forces broke through Caucasia, Germany's objective would then be solely the destruction of the Jewish element residing in the Arab sphere under the protection of British power.[26]

Hitler kept al-Husseini in Berlin, and furnished him with an enormous salary of 90,000 Reichmarks per month along with residences for himself and his entourage. Al-Husseini would broadcast radio messages to Arab listeners in Europe, urging war on the Jews. As Hitler's forces advanced in north Africa in the summer of 1942, with Palestine within reach, al-Husseini beseeched his followers to "kill the Jews wherever you find them. This pleases God, history and religion. This serves your honor, God is with you."[27]

His notorious address of November 5, 1943, in which he spoke of the Jew as "a sponge among peoples", that "sucked their blood",[28] again placed the Jews as parasitic and subhuman, as uniquely evil, a mortal threat to the world, and fit only for extermination. The parallels with Nazi depictions were unmissable. His speech could have been penned by Hitler himself.

Al-Husseini sent a birthday telegram to Heinrich Himmler, who commanded the SS, established the mobile killing squads that slaughtered millions in Eastern Europe and oversaw construction of the death camps. He received a return telegram from Himmler on the anniversary of the Balfour Declaration, in which Himmler told al-Husseini that Nazi Germany "closely follows the struggle of the freedom-seeking Arabs – and particularly in Palestine – against the Jewish invaders", which "creates the firm foundation between Germany and freedom-seeking Muslims around the world".[29]

Al-Husseini went beyond radio propaganda and hob-knobbing

with the Nazi leadership. At the invitation of the Chief of Staff of the SS Main Office, Gottlob Berger, al-Husseini travelled to Bosnia where he assisted in the recruitment of Bosnian Muslims to the SS to reinforce the war against Soviet Russia and the Jews. Berger reported that the "visit of the Grand Mufti of Jerusalem had had an extraordinarily successful impact" on recruitment.[30] The unit participated in the massacre of civilians in Bosnia and volunteered to hunt for hiding Jews in Croatia.

Addressing the imams of the Bosnian SS, al-Husseini explained, "Islam and National Socialism are close to each other in the struggle against Judaism. Nearly a third of the Qur'an deals with the Jews. It has demanded that all Muslims watch the Jews and fight them wherever they find them."[31]

A particularly chilling example of al-Husseini's hand in the destruction of European Jewry involved the deportation of 1,260 Jewish children from Bialystock in Poland. The International Red Cross had come close to brokering an exchange of the children for German prisoners of war, in an arrangement apparently favored by senior Nazis including Adolf Eichmann and Himmler. The children had been plucked from the corpse-strewn Bialystock ghetto and transported to the Theresienstadt Camp. During their long journey to the camp, the children, who had witnessed the mass shootings of their families at the Pietrasze Fields, asked their chaperones if they should jump from the train. But they were assured that the danger had passed for them and they soon arrived at the Camp where they were kept apart from the adult inmates in readiness for the exchange. Upon learning that the children would be sent onto Palestine, al-Husseini intervened. The exchange collapsed. The Auschwitz log records that the 1,260 children along with 53 Czech chaperones arrived at the camp on October 7, 1943 and were all gassed the same day.[32]

Al-Husseini was indicted after the war but never faced a war crimes trial for inciting, recruiting and interceding in support of the Nazi killing machine. His legacy is a profound one. He lives on as a symbol of Islamic antisemitism, of the deathly fusion of ancient scripture and modern political grievances, as a flagbearer of 20th century political Islam in its various forms; and as the archetypical unbending anti-Zionist whose ability to reason, accommodate or seek peace is overwhelmed by an irrational, irrepressible hatred.

His impact on the course of Zionism cannot be overstated. Leaving aside his collaboration, at the highest levels, with a regime that nearly achieved the total destruction of European Jewry, al-Husseini's rejection of the Peel Commission Partition Plan, his absolute insistence on an end to Jewish migration and land purchases thwarted the creation of a Jewish state prior to the Holocaust, with catastrophic consequences. To many Palestinian leaders who succeeded him, he remains the model of resistance to the Jews and other perceived western interlopers. His self-serving appeals to pan-Arabism, propensity to inflame the street with claims of Jewish plots to destroy Islamic holy sites, and campaigns to internationalize the conflict against Zionism through alliances with despotic regimes, have all become mainstays of the Palestinian national movement.

Haj Amin al-Husseini meeting leader of the SS, Heinrich Himmler (Bundesarchiv, Kurt Alber, Creative Commons).

Haj Amin al-Husseini during a visit to Bosnia to recruit Muslims soldiers to the Nazi SS (Creative Commons).

Al-Husseini meeting with Hitler
(Bundesarchiv, Heinrich Hoffmann, Creative Commons).

HAAVARA

A curious episode in both the history of Nazi Germany and the Zionist movement involves the so-called "Haavara" (Transfer) Agreement concluded between representatives of the Jewish Agency for Palestine, the Zionist Organization in Germany and the German Ministry for Economics in August 1933, shortly after Hitler's rise to power.

The substance of the agreement was that German Jews wishing to leave for Palestine could retain some of their assets by transferring funds into the German bank account of a special-purpose company, and the funds would then be used to purchase German goods for export to Palestine. Once the goods were sold in Palestine, the German-Jewish refugees depositing the funds would receive the proceeds less a healthy cut for the Nazi Government. In essence, the agreement allowed the German Jews to ransom themselves, and escape with their lives and part of their assets.

As a written agreement between Zionists and the Nazis, Haavara is nevertheless viewed with some controversy. The agreement served numerous purposes. For the Nazis it sought to undermine a growing international boycott of its goods over its antisemitic policies. While the transactions contemplated under the agreement were really a transfer of private German-Jewish assets from Germany to Palestine, on the face of it, it involved the importation of German goods by Jews in Palestine. How could a boycott of German goods hold when the Jews of Palestine were themselves importing German goods? For the Zionist leadership, the agreement offered a way of getting German Jews out of the clutches of Nazism and inducing them to migrate to Palestine. And for the German Jews who participated in the agreement, it offered them a way out of Germany, while enabling them to retain part of their wealth.

We have seen that in response to persecution, the first Jewish response was always to reach accommodation with their oppressor. Haavara was just such an attempt. Through their history of exile, the Jews had encountered all manner of antisemites in Europe and the Middle East. Therefore they initially reacted to Nazism with their usual catalogue of reactions to a perceived threat, from taking flight to seeking dialogue and negotiations in the hope of alleviating harm, and gritting teeth and solemnly expecting to outlive yet another oppressor. But Nazism was unique. While its antisemitic nature was known, its unremitting, insatiable commitment to the total destruction of the people could not be contemplated.

Ultimately, the Haavara Agreement saved lives to the extent that it helped facilitate emigration and provided a practical solution to the problems Jews faced when attempting to take assets with them. It fit with the times. The Nazis always sought a solution to the "Jewish problem", and aggressively encouraging emigration of Jews from Germany was the solution at the time of the Nazi ascent to power. It was not until 1938-39 that that solution entailed looting, concentration camps and deportation. It was not until 1941 that it took the form of annihilation.

The existence of this agreement between the German Government and the Zionists, has prompted opponents of Zionism to allege actual collaboration. The former Mayor of London, Ken Livingstone referred to the Haavara Agreement in support of his view that Hitler "was supporting Zionism before he went mad and ended up killing six million Jews."[33]

The assertion that Hitler at any time "supported Zionism" is plainly ahistorical and demonstrably false. In his meeting with al-Husseini, Hitler expressly opposed a Jewish national home, which he claimed would be "nothing other than a center, in the form of a state, for the exercise of destructive influence by Jewish interests."[34] Years earlier, in his manifesto *Mein Kampf*, Hitler wrote of Zionism and the creation of a Jewish state:

> While the Zionists try to make the rest of the World believe that the national consciousness of the Jew finds its satisfaction in the creation of a Palestinian state, the Jews again slyly dupe the dumb Goyim. It doesn't even enter their heads to build up a Jewish state in Palestine for the purpose of living there; all they want is a central

organization for their international world swindler, endowed with its own sovereign rights and removed from the intervention of other states: a haven for convicted scoundrels and a university for budding crooks.[35]

Hardly the sentiments of someone "supporting Zionism". In fact, the notion that Hitler had any sympathy or support for Zionism is an absurdity entering the realm of satire. Zionism sought to win the equality of the Jew. Hitler held Jews to be subhuman. Zionism sought national liberation for the Jewish people. Hitler pursued their destruction to the end. Zionism revived the Hebrew language and sought to safeguard and enlarge Jewish culture, traditions and heritage. Hitler demanded the obliteration of any trace of Jewish influence.

Far from being an endorsement of Zionism by the Nazis, the Haavara Agreement was a cynical, opportunistic act of exploitation by the Nazi regime of innocent people who were anxious to escape the depredations of that very regime.

ASHES

The Holocaust brought no redemption or awakening. Its seemingly infinite stories of infinite evil have been presented to us over and over again in dispassionate historical texts, in Hollywood films, novellas and memoirs. All seek, and all fail to fully explain why human beings would act this way to their fellow man. What was it about the Jews that aroused such feeling that the army of a sophisticated nation would be deployed to traverse the European continent with the mission of extinguishing every last Jewish life? What discord existed in the hearts of ordinary men and women that they would shed their humanity entirely, and seize with unrelenting fury and purpose the opportunity to dispossess, humiliate and destroy their neighbors simply because they were Jewish? These are the imponderables at the heart of the Holocaust.

The Jewish national movement was well advanced long before the rise of Nazism and the Holocaust. Had it not been for the intensity of the Arab opposition to Zionism and the willingness of the British to depart from their responsibilities in the name of wider interests, the Jews would have had their home and their sanctuary long before the first anti-Jewish actions took place.

The effect of the Holocaust was to definitively prove the central thesis of Zionism. In fact, it is difficult to think of another event proving another political theory so starkly and unequivocally. The notion that assimilation, integration and loyalty would be the salvation of the Jews of Europe was proved a farce.

David Ben-Gurion, now the head of the Jewish Agency, said that "what Zionist propaganda for years could not do," being to convince Jews of their utter vulnerability, "disaster has done overnight."[36]

One Holocaust survivor who made passage to Palestine said that the local Jews viewed the survivors as "human wreckage."[37] As story after story, true or false, emerged of Jews obediently walking into the gas chambers or climbing into the graves they had just dug for themselves, a common response to survivors emerged in Palestine, one which Elie Wiesel characterized as being, "six million of you let yourselves be led like lambs to the slaughter."[38] One survivor, Yehudah Layb Gersht, observed that "their Jewish spinal cord was severed by their misery."[39]

The stories of Jewish resistance in camps and ghettoes, the formation of partisans operating behind enemy lines, of daring escape from certain death, had not yet fully emerged. The single narrative was one of Jews showing no fight whatsoever. The Jews of Palestine, meanwhile, had lived by virtue of their enterprise and courage. They had smuggled guns for patrols against Arab militias, erected the tower and stockade by night, and formed their own militias to challenge the British and retaliate against the Arabs. Returning to hallowed lands, tilling the soil, acting in self-defense had given the Jews a wholly new character, one far closer to the forebears in the land than their contemporaries in Europe. Arguably, it was not until the trial of Adolf Eichmann in 1961, for his leading role in the Holocaust, that the Jews who had been in Palestine during the war came to understand the full extent of the horrors and just how helpless any civilian population would have been in the face of such sophistication and unceasing evil.

Zionism after the Holocaust was hardened further still. It could not have been otherwise. If the pogroms in Kishinev and Hebron led to Jewish awakenings, an event on the scale of the Holocaust would have that effect a thousand times over. The Holocaust had shown how determined were the enemies of the Jewish people and how alone were the Jews in an international system dominated by self-interest and moral paralysis.

Zionism now combined the hearty experience in the land with the ghoulish image of what they could again become and what the world had stood by and let them be. The ethos of the Zionist now became – A Jew could still be hit but now he will hit back.

9

ISRAEL

In a long, ostensibly stream-of-consciousness letter to US President Franklin D. Roosevelt, the Saudi ruler, King Abdul Aziz Ibn Saud made the case against a Jewish state, beseeching the President to "stop the flow of [Jewish] migration to Palestine", and to "prevent completely the sale of lands to them."[1] Laced with references to the Jews as "would-be murderers" whose "treacherous behavior", "has been the cause of many troubles in the past," Ibn Saud's letter came in April 1943, at a time when the genocide of the Jews was proceeding with industrial efficiency.

Once Germany was defeated, the cloak of war was gradually lifted, fully revealing the scale of the horrors to which the European Jews had been subjected. But even this could not dislodge the White Paper with its restrictions on Jewish migration to Palestine. Nor could it cause a thaw in the intensity of Arab anti-Zionism.

Once al-Husseini, the collaborator, concluded his business in Europe, he was welcomed in Egypt as a patriot. The founder of the Muslim Brotherhood, Hassan al-Banna lauded al-Husseini as a "hero who challenged an empire and fought Zionism with the help of Hitler and Germany."[2] Al-Husseini was soon installed as leader of the Arab Higher Committee and of the Palestine People's Party.

The British remained steadfast in their Palestine policy too. They continued to pursue a middling path that they hoped would appease the Arab and Islamic world but without completely repudiating their legal and moral commitments to the Jews, which would diminish Britain's international standing.

All the while, the Jews who had survived the killing fields or the death camps were now confined to displaced persons camps, sometimes in the very camps where they had nearly met their deaths, and often shoulder to shoulder with the very men who had hunted them.

In June 1945, US President Truman sent his representative on the Intergovernmental Commission on Refugees, Earl Harrison, to Europe to report on the condition of Jews in these displaced persons camps. *The Harrison Report*, as it came to be known, told of the cruel indifference with which the surviving European Jews were now being stored:

> ... Many Jewish displaced persons are living under guard behind barbed-wire fences, in camps of several descriptions, including some of the most notorious of the concentration camps, amidst crowded, frequently unsanitary and generally grim conditions, in complete idleness.
>
> ... There are pathetic malnutrition cases. The death rate has been high since liberation. One Army chaplain, a Rabbi personally attended, since liberation, 23,000 burials (90% Jews) at Bergen Belsen alone, one of the largest and most vicious of the concentration camps.
>
> ... many of the Jewish displaced persons, had no clothing other than their concentration camp garb – a rather hideous striped pajama effect – while others, to their chagrin, were obliged to wear German SS uniforms.

> The most absorbing story of these Nazi and war victims concerns relatives – wives, husbands, parents, children. Most of them have been separated for three, four, five years and they cannot understand why the liberators should not have undertaken immediately the organized effort to reunite family groups.[3]

Harrison also observed the desperate desire of the survivors to leave the camps and Europe behind and noted that "Palestine is definitely and preeminently the first choice" of destination.[4] He recommended that given the scale and urgency of the deprivation to which he bore witness, "… the issue of Palestine must be faced." "Now that such large numbers are no longer involved and if there is any genuine sympathy for what these survivors have endured," Harrison wrote, "some reasonable extension of or modification of the British White Paper of 1939 ought to be possible without too serious repercussions."

The trauma inflicted on the Jews by their non-Jewish neighbors had been so profound that they now yearned for separation, to be in the company of their own, among whom they could seek to reclaim some semblance of normalcy and dignity. Those Jews who had sought to return to former homes to reclaim property or learn of the fate of loved ones were confronted by antisemitism undiminished by the bloodletting of the war.

A doctor working in the camps observed that for those who had lost their families, the most powerful compulsion was to "find refuge in the Jewish nation", being a surrogate for their lost kin. Settling in Palestine was now the only family reunion they could hope for.[5]

Samuel Gringauz, a survivor and displaced persons camp inmate articulated what Zionism now meant to the remnants of European Jewry. It was their sole hope which could no longer be delayed or negotiated away. "Life in the Diaspora for the Jewish displaced persons is synonymous with recurrence. No sociological argument can obliterate from their minds what experience has stamped on it ... Neither equality of rights, nor a constitution, nor patriotism is security against persecution ... It can happen again. And therefore we demand of you to build up Palestine not only for us but as an ultimate place of refuge (for the Jewish people as a whole)."[6]

But the British were unmoving. A Cabinet committee was appointed on 28 August 1945 to address the question of Palestine, at least in the short-term. The decision that followed was to continue to restrict Jewish migration on the basis of the White Paper.[7]

At a press conference on 13 November 1945, British Foreign Secretary Ernest Bevin gave a remarkable insight into how unhinged British policy on Palestine had become. He told the conference: "I am very anxious that Jews shall not in Europe over-emphasize their racial position. If the Jews, with all their sufferings, want to get too much at the head of the queue, you will have the danger of another antisemitic reaction through it all."[8] The "racial position" of the Jews had been made evident by those who hunted and killed them on the very basis of their race. Yet, Bevin now reduced the survivors to bothersome queue-jumpers and suggested that lethal antisemitism was a reaction to Jewish conduct.

Chaim Weizmann responded to Bevin that the Jews were accustomed to standing in the front of queues and had already done so at the gates of Auschwitz and Treblinka.[9]

Bevin's refusal to grant entry visas to Palestine for survivors was greeted with a renewed sense of loss by them. One camp employee noted that the day of Bevin's announcement that Palestine remained barred to the survivors "was a day of mourning."[10]

The reason for British obstinacy was becoming evident. A Cabinet memorandum dated January 1947 spoke of the "center of gravity" of oil production that had shifted to Arab lands and the impact that support for Jewish statehood would have on such interests.[11] To add to the calculations of the British, the risk that violence would engulf the Arab street and destabilize the region owing to events in Palestine, was constant or was at least made to seem as such.

But the Jews were now determined to throw off their passivity and apply their own pressure to influence British policy. Displaced persons camp inmates instituted strikes. While at a press conference in New York, Ben-Gurion foreshadowed a new Jewish resistance, declaring that if the British intended to maintain their restrictions on Jewish migration to Palestine via the White Paper, they would have to do so with "constant and brutal force".[12]

RESISTANCE

There had been a time when Palestine animated British idealism. Now it was a nuisance to be shed. Europe still smoldered from the crimes of Nazism, another aggressive totalitarianism was rising in the form of Stalinism, and new strategic opportunities were to be found in the Arab world. The Paris Conference and post-World War I treaty-making, the Balfour Declaration and Weizmann's war heroics all seemed like ancient curiosities.

At the beginning of 1947, some 18 months after the end of the war, 210,000 Jews still languished in the camps. That year, the British commandeered the Exodus, the ship carrying 4,500 Holocaust survivors for Palestine, and sent the passengers back to Europe. The Jewish leaders in the displaced persons camps declared, "nothing will deter us from Palestine."[13]

We have seen how violence, or even the apprehension of it, tilted and swayed British policy-making in Palestine. Now the Zionists, feeling they had little to lose, were replicating the tactics of the Arabs in the hope of achieving their own political transformation and dislodging a Britain that had become morally dubious and indifferent.

Since 1920, following the Nebi Musa riots, and particularly following the massacre in Hebron in 1929, the Jews in Palestine had organized their defenses. Beginning as detached units of young pioneers with rifles guarding outlying communities from Arab bandits, they soon matured into a basic militia capable of carrying out operations, recruiting and training, smuggling arms, and more than giving the Arabs a run for their money.

The partition of Palestine in 1922 through the creation of Transjordan had caused a rupture in Zionism between the mainstream movement, then led by Weizmann, and the revisionists led by Jabotinsky. The Jewish militias soon organized on similar lines, with the Haganah serving as the main defense force, while the Irgun was formed by members of Jabotinsky's movement. Eventually a third and most reactionary force emerged as a splinter of the Irgun. This third group was led by one of the Irgun's former commanders, Avraham Stern, and came to be known as Lehi or the Stern Gang.

The revisionists had never accepted that territorial concessions were either just or a recipe for peaceful coexistence with the Arabs. They remained territorial maximalists demanding a Jewish state on both sides of the River Jordan, as depicted in the seal of the Irgun. Having seen partitions and white papers reduce the land and virtually extinguish hopes of a Jewish state in any borders, they were resolved to removing the British by force.

On 6 November 1944, Lord Moyne, the British Resident Minister in Cairo arrived at his official residence to find two Palestinian Jews of the Stern Gang, Eliahu Bet-Tsuri and Eliahu Hakim waiting near the entrance. One of the men approached Moyne's vehicle, thrust his pistol through the open window and fired three times, killing Moyne.

The killing appalled the world. Chaim Weizmann said that the death hurt him more than the loss of his own son during the War.[14] Churchill, aghast, declared that for the sake of Zionism, "these wicked activities must cease, and those responsible for them must be destroyed root and branch."[15]

The condemnation of the Jewish Agency was the strongest of all. They called on the Jews of Palestine to "cast out the members of this destructive band, deprive them of all refuge and shelter, to resist their threats, and render all assistance to the [British] in the prevention of terrorist acts and in the eradication of the terrorist organization."[16]

The deeds were even stronger. The Haganah declared war on the Irgun and the Stern Gang, providing hundreds of names of members to the British, who promptly arrested them. Averting a potential crisis of Zionism, the leadership sought to prevent the movement from entering the abyss of violence and retribution.

They had long charted a course founded in diplomacy, moderation and compromise. They now had to ensure that the vision of Herzl did not "end in the smoke of assassins' pistols", in the words of Churchill.[17]

Recognizing Zionism had arrived at a crucial moment, Weizmann spoke with his usual clarity and profoundness. "Assassination, ambush, kidnapping, the murder of innocent men, are alien to the spirit of our movement," he declared. "We came to Palestine to build, not to destroy; terror distorts the essence of Zionism. It insults our history; it mocks the ideals for which a Jewish society must stand; it sullies our banner; it compromises our appeal to the world's liberal conscience."[18]

But the marginalization of the Stern Gang and the Irgun from mainstream Zionism did not cause them to disband, nor did they repudiate the use of targeted killings to achieve their political aims. The attacks continued. On 29 June 1946, the British carried out an operation throughout Palestine which led to the arrests and incarceration of over 2,000 Zionist leaders and officials, in what came to be known as "Black Sabbath".

Ben-Gurion, in Paris at the time, was one of the few major leaders to evade arrest. While in Paris, he happened to be staying at the same hotel as Ho Chi Minh, the Vietnamese nationalist leader. Having established the genial bond of freedom-fighters seeking a homeland, Ho Chi Minh suggested to Ben-Gurion that he establish a Jewish Government in Exile and would even afford him a headquarters in the north of Vietnam. Ben-Gurion politely declined.[19]

In spite of the incarceration of the Zionist leadership and the disruption of the Irgun and Stern Gang through Haganah cooperation with the British, the pressure on the British was mounting. President Truman issued a public rebuke of Britain's continued confinement of Holocaust survivors in Europe, and its refusal to issue even 100,000 entry permits to Palestine for the most vulnerable survivors.[20] The callous treatment of the displaced persons added to British fatigue with Palestine and public pressure for a solution mounted. The cost to the British taxpayers was mounting too. Administering the Mandate had cost over £23,500,000.[21]

A week prior to the "Black Sabbath" arrests the Irgun had sought to impose a greater toll still. On 22 July 1946, it carried out the bombing of the King David Hotel in Jerusalem, which the British had used as the headquarters of the British Mandate government and intelligence apparatus in Palestine.

The Irgun, and its political successors, maintained and still maintain, that an unheeded warning to evacuate was delivered 27 minutes before the blast. The building was never evacuated and 91 people were killed when milk churns packed with explosives were detonated in the building's basement cafe.

Among the dead were 28 Britons, 41 Arabs and 17 Jews. The attack shocked the Jews of Palestine, enraged the people of Britain and prompted unequivocal denunciations from the Zionist leadership. Ben-Gurion called the Irgun the "enemy of the Jewish people." The Jewish Agency called the bombing a "base and unparalleled act by a gang of criminals."[22]

The financial, political and now human toll of the Mandate had grown intolerable for the British. At a Cabinet meeting on 14 February 1947, it was resolved that the question of Palestine would be handed to the United Nations, the successor to the

League of Nations.

The author Evelyn Waugh said that Bevin's abandonment of the Mandate was the product of "cowardice, sloth and parsimony."[23]

On 25 February 1947, the British Foreign Secretary Bevin addressed the British Parliament to explain his decision. His speech showed that Britain had reached the end of its productive capacity in Palestine. The Balfour Declaration, no longer the moral guide for British policy-making in Palestine, was an albatross. To Bevin, it had brought false hope of a homeland to come for the Jews and aroused unerring fury among the Arabs. "All I want is a settlement," Bevin proclaimed in his irritation and fatigue. "And I want a settlement because this is one of those sore spots in the Middle East that may, if not settled, lead to much wider trouble."[24] He lashed out at the Americans for their concern for the fate of the Jews wallowing season on season in the old-new camps of Europe. Referring to the envoy President Truman had sent to report on the conditions in the displaced persons camps, Bevin railed: "A person named Earl Harrison went out to their zone in Germany collecting certain information, and a report was issued. I must say it really destroyed the basis of good feeling that we – the Colonial Secretary and I – were endeavoring to produce in the Arab States, and it set the whole thing back."[25]

The pitiful state of Britain's Palestine policy and its abdication of the historic responsibilities it had willingly accepted, was laid bare by Bevin in his response to a question from a parliamentary colleague. Bevin was asked what he understood by the word "national" in the phrase "Jewish national home". After all, it was precisely that which the British had through the Balfour Declaration, Paris Peace Conference and League of Nations vowed to help create. "I am sorry that I cannot give an accurate definition," Bevin answered, "and Balfour is dead."[26]

TWO STATES FOR TWO PEOPLES

With the responsibility for solving the Palestine problem now before the United Nations, a special 11-member committee, known as the United Nations Special Committee on Palestine (UNSCOP) was established to propose a solution. In a prelude to what would become a recurring theme in contemporary Palestinian politics, the Arab Higher Committee called a boycott of UNSCOP's proceedings and did not appear before the Committee. The position of the Arabs of Palestine had remained unchanged – 'no' to a Jewish state, 'no' to further Jewish migration, and 'no' to Jewish land purchases. They therefore saw little merit in cooperating with the UN's inquiry. Henry Cattan, a representative of the Arab Palestinians, considered the boycott to be "unfortunate", since it allowed Weizmann, Ben Gurion and others to be heard by the Committee "without contradiction from the Arab side."[27]

Nevertheless, the Arab position was put, rather forcefully, in Beirut by the Lebanese Foreign Minister Frangie. Frangie considered the Balfour Declaration and British Mandate for Palestine to be "null and valueless", and demanded that "all Jewish migration to Palestine stop immediately", along with "land transfers" [to Jews], and called for the creation of "an independent Arab government" in Palestine. Once again seasoning Arab demands with the veiled threat of further violence, the Arab delegation asserted that "the responsibility for the disturbances which might result throughout the Middle East will rest solely with the Zionist organizations."[28]

UNSCOP tabled their report to the United Nations on 3 September 1947. They had failed to reach a unanimous position and presented a majority proposal (favored by 7 of its members) calling once again for partition of the remaining area of Palestine into a Jewish state and an Arab state. A minority view (endorsed by 3 members) called for the creation of an independent Federal state within which the Arab and Jewish communities would each have a degree of political autonomy, but in which the Arab majority would dominate. None of the UNSCOP members supported the Arab demand for a unitary Arab state, which would give no recognition whatsoever to Jewish national self-determination and make no provision for it. One delegate abstained. The majority position adopted by Sweden, Uruguay, Canada, Peru, the Netherlands, Guatemala and Czechoslovakia was that both sides had valid claims to the land and such claims had become "irreconcilable". "Regardless of the historical origins of the conflict," the report stated, "the rights and wrongs, there are now in Palestine 650,000 Jews and 1,200,000 Arabs who are dissimilar in their ways of living and separated by political interests. Only by means of partition can these conflicting national aspirations find substantial expression and qualify both peoples to take their places as independent nations."[29]

The new Partition Plan excluded Jerusalem which was to become a Corpus Separatum under international supervision. It was Zionism without Zion.

Not only had Jerusalem been the ancient capital of Judea and had been the object of Jewish prayer and devoted custom ever since, but by 1947, Jerusalem was home to 100,000 Jews. The Jews had been a majority in the city since 1860. Therefore, aside from keeping the ancient Jewish capital from Jewish sovereignty, it placed a considerable portion of the Palestinian Jews outside the borders of the new state.

But as they had done at every turn, the Zionist leadership was prepared to accept less. With eyes fixed firmly on the goal of a Jewish national home, a sanctuary, a return of the exiled, and a place where Jewish national life and creativity could again flourish, the precise contours of the borders, even the exclusion of both Jerusalem and Hebron, were secondary considerations. Now with hundreds of thousands languishing in displaced persons camps for a third year following the death camps, the Zionist leadership acceded and accepted, cautiously and reluctantly, the partition proposal.

The American Zionist leader Abba Hillel Silver, considered that partition was a "very heavy sacrifice", but one the Jewish people would be prepared to make.[30]

On 2 October 1947, a month after UNSCOP had recommended partition, Ben-Gurion addressed the Assembly of Palestine Jews. A Federal state, as proposed by a minority of the UNSCOP members, would not deliver a Jewish homeland or a national return, he said. It was founded, Ben-Gurion asserted, in the "denial of our age-long connection with Palestine" and meant, owing to the earlier restrictions on Jewish migration, "Arab precedence in all things, even in immigration, and in short, produces an Arab State in the false feathers of bi-nationalism."[31]

Partition, foremost in Ben-Gurion's mind, meant the end of the White Paper, "with its locked gates and its racial discrimination".[32] Arabs had freely migrated to the land in search of new economic opportunities, but British policy had caused the seemingly perpetual obstruction of the development of the land by the Jews. Partition would end all that.

In a private letter, Ben-Gurion considered that partition "would truly be the beginning of the redemption."[33] Foremost in Ben-Gurion's mind was security. He knew that with the departure of the British now imminent, civil war between the Arabs and the Jews and a regional war involving the neighboring Arab states, was likely. "Security is our chief problem," he told the Assembly. "And not a single Jewish unit exists".[34]

But by the end of 1947, the Jews in Palestine were prepared for small arms combat. While totally lacking in airpower and heavy guns, they had accumulated some 17,600 rifles, 2,700 sten-guns and a thousand machine-guns. A fighting force of around 30,000 was assembled, and hastily trained. "We are preparing for D-Day" he wrote.[35]

Meanwhile, the partition proposal of UNSCOP was being steered through the United Nations by an Ad Hoc Committee chaired by the Australian statesman Dr Herbert Vere ("Doc") Evatt.

The result was United Nations General Assembly Resolution 181 (II), which put the Partition Plan to a vote of each member state of the United Nations. The Resolution called for the creation of "independent Arab and Jewish States and the Special International Regime for the City of Jerusalem" to come into effect by "no later than 1 October 1948". The Resolution further provided for the termination of the Mandate, the withdrawal of the British, a guarantee of unimpaired access to holy sites, free access to Jerusalem for citizens of the Jewish and Arab States, and an economic union between the States, including a common currency.

Viewed in the context of the still-unresolved conflict, Resolution 181 (II) offered a solution and an alternative to perpetual war. It would put an end to internal hostilities, achieve separation such as would preserve the national aspirations of Jews and Arabs in Palestine, while heading-off the prospect of invasion by the surrounding states.

The Arabs went into diplomatic overdrive in opposition. A US State Department officer complained of Arab "blackmail" and threats.[36] British and US oil companies, concerned only for their interests, backed the Arab position.[37]

The Soviet position was unclear. US intelligence assessed that the Soviets would be opposed to any form of independent Jewish statehood, and would view such a state as a "Zionist tool of the West".[38]

Then on May 14, 1947, the Soviet delegate to the United Nations, Andrei Gromyko ascended to the podium to address the General Assembly of the UN. Known for his diplomatic savvy and grim bearing, Gromyko gave an oration that virtually no one had foreseen. He reviewed the history of the Palestine question, its aims and its failures, before considering the condition of the Jews.

The position of the Soviet Union on the Holocaust had been an uneasy one, dominated by distortion, minimization and obfuscation. The fact that great numbers of Soviet citizens had aided the invaders in their war against the Soviet Union, in some cases forming collaborationist militias and armies in their bid to escape Soviet tyranny, made a mockery of Stalinist pretenses to a national unity. The Soviet authorities were also loathe to admit that a genocide had taken place on Soviet soil, often with the support of regular Soviet citizens reared on the antisemitic fables of the Soviet and Tsarist regimes.

But here Gromyko confronted what had happened to the

Jews, albeit while skillfully shifting the blame and the burden of guilt west of the Soviet lands.

> During the last war, the Jewish people underwent exceptional sorrow and suffering. Without any exaggeration, this sorrow and suffering are indescribable. It is difficult to express them in dry statistics on the Jewish victims of the fascist aggressors. The Jews in territories where the Hitlerites held sway were subjected to almost complete physical annihilation. The total number of members of the Jewish population who perished at the hands of the nazi executioners is estimated at approximately six million. Only about a million and a half Jews in Western Europe survived the war.
>
> But these figures, although they give an idea of the number of victims of the fascist aggressors among the Jewish people, give no idea of the difficulties in which large numbers of Jewish people found themselves after the war.
>
> Large numbers of the surviving Jews of Europe were deprived of their countries, their homes and their means of existence. Hundreds of thousands of Jews are wandering about in various countries of Europe in search of means of existence and in search of shelter. A large number of them are in camps for displaced persons and are still continuing to undergo great privations.
>
> It may well be asked if the United Nations, in view of the difficult situation of hundreds of thousands of the surviving Jewish population, can fail to show an interest in the situation of these people, torn away from their countries and their homes. The United Nations cannot and must not regard this situation with indifference, since this would be incompatible with the high principles proclaimed in its Charter, which provide for the defense of human rights, irrespective of race, religion or sex. The time has come to help these people, not by word, but by deeds.

Before offering a solution, Gromyko ruminated on the solemn duty to recognize the rights of a people whose very right to exist on this earth had been withdrawn:

> Past experience, particularly during the Second World War, shows that no western European State was able to provide adequate assistance for the Jewish people in defending its rights and its very existence from the violence of the Hitlerites and their allies.
>
> The fact that no western European State has been able to ensure the defense of the elementary rights of the Jewish people, and to safeguard it against the violence of the fascist executioners, explains the aspirations of the Jews to establish their own State. It would be unjust not to take this into consideration and to deny the right of the Jewish people to realize this aspiration. It would be unjustifiable to deny this right to the Jewish people, particularly in view of all it has undergone during the Second World War.[39]

The preferred Soviet solution was a Federal state. This was a paradoxical position as a state in which the Jews were a minority would not grant them their national rights, but Gromyko noted that if relations between the Jews and the Arabs in Palestine should make a single state impractical, the Soviets would be prepared to support partition.

Gromyko's speech brought elation in the Jewish world. Israeli statesmen-in-waiting, Abba Eban and Moshe Sharett called it "a windfall" and an "ideological revolution".[40]

The speech was not what the Arabs had anticipated and they set to work attempting to torpedo the partition proposal, in one final diplomatic push to prevent the creation of a Jewish state before resorting to war.

The months before the matter came to a vote of the UN General Assembly were marked by a frenzy of lobbying, coercion, threats, bribes and pledges whispered, cabled and phoned at all hours and to all manner of influencer and potential interlocutor.

Finally, on November 29, 1947 the nations of the world cast their votes on Resolution 181 (II), which proposed two states in the Mandate of Palestine. The Resolution passed by 33 votes to 13 with 10 abstentions. Joining the Muslim-majority countries in voting "no", were Cuba and India. In a rare moment of accord before the Cold War would truly consume international affairs, the Soviet Union and the United States both voted in favor. Britain, its administration of the Mandate ending in a whimper, now abstained in the partition vote.

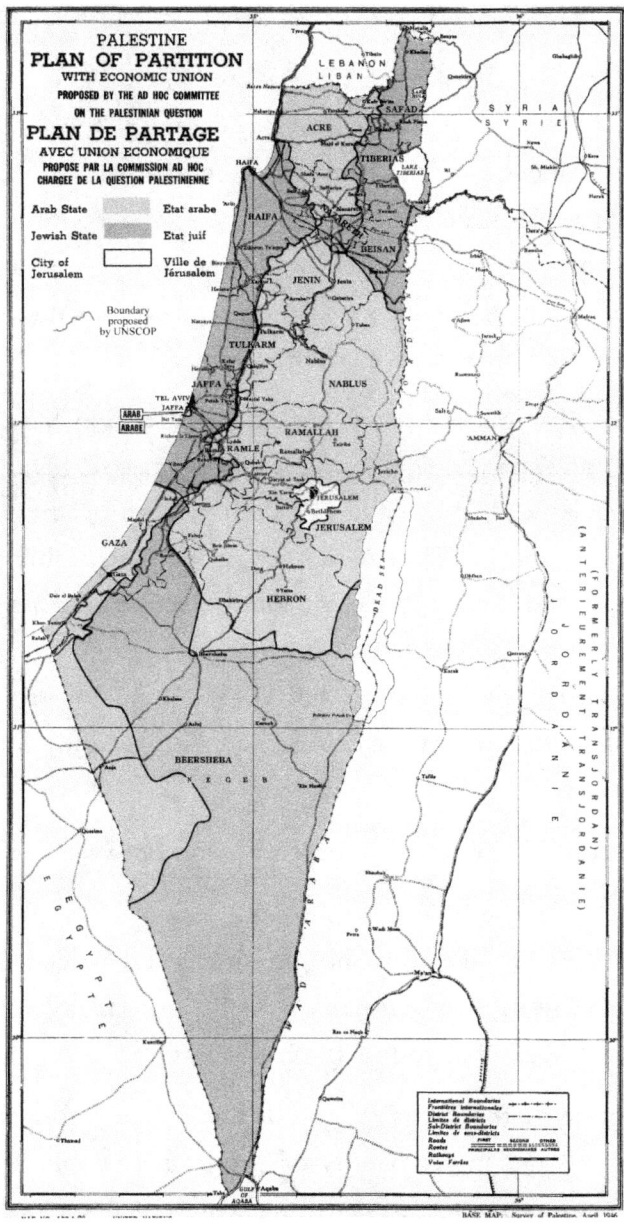

United Nations Plan of Partition with economic union, which was adopted by the General Assembly on 29 November 1947, (Public Domain).

THE ROAD TO WAR

The Arab reaction to the Resolution was characteristically unambiguous. One by one, the Arab states denounced the Resolution, vowed to be unbound by it, claimed the right to use armed force to prevent its implementation, and disclaimed any responsibility for the consequences of the war they would themselves now unleash. Having failed in the diplomatic game, the Arabs now openly declared their intention to destroy Jewish statehood by force.

Faisal al Saud of Saudi Arabia charged that the UN Charter "and all the covenants preceding it" had been destroyed. Next, Syria: "The Charter is dead. But it did not die a natural death, and you all know who is guilty". Yemen "did not consider itself bound" by the Resolution and "reserved its freedom of action". Iraq similarly "reserved freedom of action towards its implementation." Syria again: "Let the consequences be on the heads of others, not on ours."[41] The Arab Higher Committee in Palestine called the Resolution "a declaration of war".

The reaction of the Jewish world was one of weary euphoria, disbelief, open joy and veiled trepidation.

In Palestine, Jews spilled out onto the streets and danced through the night. Elsewhere in the Jewish diaspora, the news from New York was met with "sheer jubilation and wonderment".[42]

The adoption of the Partition Plan by the United Nations stands as a momentous day in the history of the Jewish people. It was a moment of national rebirth, of collective achievement and collective redemption. But it was also experienced on a deeply personal level. The promise of statehood instantly transformed how a Jew viewed himself. For a people who had etched every tragedy and anguish into their national memory, the occasion was felt not merely in its time but as a moment in history. One could almost sense a physical transformation in the Jew as the resolution passed – no longer supine, no longer hunched, no longer waiting for the blow.

Amos Oz, the great Israeli literary figure experienced the moment in the company of his father. He wrote of that night:

> "From the moment we have our own state [his father said to him], you will never be bullied just because you are a Jew and because Jews are so-and-sos. Not that. Never again. From tonight that's finished here. Forever." I reached out sleepily to touch his face, just below his high forehead, and all of a sudden instead of his glasses my fingers met tears. Never in my life, before or after that night, not even when my mother died, did I see my father cry. And in fact I didn't see him cry that night, either. Only my left hand saw.[43]

Moshe Dayan, who would become a commander of Jewish forces in the coming war, reflected in his memoirs:

> I felt in my bones the victory of Judaism, which for two thousand years of exile from the Land of Israel had withstood persecutions, the Spanish Inquisition, pogroms, anti-Jewish decrees, restrictions, and the mass slaughter by the Nazis in our own generation, and had reached the fulfilment of its age-old yearning – the return to a free and independent Zion.[44]

But there was nothing in the story of Zionism, or indeed in the history of the Jewish people, that would indicate that adoption of the Partition Plan by the United Nations, would lead to the orderly transition to Jewish statehood that the Resolution provided for.

The Balfour Declaration had not led to statehood. Neither had Jewish development of the land or lawful settlement. At each turn, the fulfilment of Zionism had been foiled, blown off its apparent course, or muscled into concessions that left the movement with less land and more spilled blood.

The day after the Resolution was passed, on November 30, 1947, Palestine was at civil war. That day, Arab gunmen ambushed two Jewish passenger buses near Petah Tikva, killing seven people. The Arab Higher Committee called a three-day general strike and protests for the following day which resulted in widespread looting and burning of Jewish shops in Jerusalem. In Tel Aviv, Arab rioters attacked Jewish civilians. Isolated settlements in the Negev desert and the Hebron hills were besieged, would-be looters at the ready. Buses were ambushed. In some instances, Jewish passengers were separated from Arabs and shot. Snipers took potshots at Jews in Jerusalem.

In this instance, the Jews were not passive victims. They had expected war and though poorly armed, they were ready. In the ensuing skirmishes the brother of Moshe Dayan, Zorik, died in battle. On the Arab side, the nephew of Al-Husseini, Abd al-Qadir was killed as well.

In April 1948, the violence reached a peak. On April 9, Irgun and Stern Gang forces sought to clear the Arab village of Deir Yassin, outside Jerusalem to prevent further attacks on Jewish transports along the adjacent road by Arab fighters embedded in the village. After the fierce urban combat had ended, reports quickly spread of a massacre of prisoners by Jewish fighters and other atrocities.

On April 13, Arab gunmen opened fire with machine-guns and petrol bombs on a medical convoy carrying doctors and nurses to the Hadassah Hospital on Mount Scopus in Jerusalem. 79 people were shot or incinerated, including the director of the hospital Dr Chaim Yassky, a noted ophthalmologist. Born in the city of Kishinev, seven years before the pogrom of 1903, Yassky had withstood the mob violence there and later in Odessa, before falling in Jerusalem.

The Jewish Chronicle reported on the massacre of doctors and nurses as an act of "insensate folly and wickedness which could strike down men and women engaged in such work ... which must benefit Jew and Arab alike, and spread improved methods of healing throughout Palestine and the Middle East."[45]

THE MANDATE ENDS

As Palestine moved nearer the abyss, Britain abandoned the Mandate. Under Resolution 181 (II) it was compelled to terminate the Mandate and withdraw its forces by no later than 1 August 1948, but the British now hastened for the exits.

By the evening of May 14, 1948, the British were gone.

On the same day, the Jewish leadership in Palestine convened in Tel Aviv and decided that they would declare statehood and form a provincial government. "Politics predominantly abhors a vacuum",[46] Ben-Gurion had told the leadership the month before the partition vote and he was determined that British power should be replaced immediately with the Jewish state.

One immediate question now stood before the founding fathers – what to name their new country. Various names were considered including Zion, Herzliya, Judea but each failed to rise to the magnitude of the moment. Then the suggestion of "Israel" was put. There is little by way of historical record of these deliberations and whether it was Moshe Sharrett or Ben-Gurion who proposed "Israel", remains in doubt. Sharrett had used the formulation "State of Israel" in a speech in 1946, while Ben-Gurion had generally spoken of the "Jewish state".[47] Walter Eytan recalled that "the moment the name was proclaimed, everyone realized instinctively it could in fact have no other."[48]

Indeed, no name could have captured the essence of the Zionist project and the Jewish national resurrection better. On the oldest relic attesting to the existence of a Hebrew-speaking people, the Pharaoh Merenptah had proclaimed: "Israel is laid waste, its seed is not." Now Israel had risen from the ashes. Its seed had been restored to their ancient homeland. Zionism had been fulfilled. The Jews had won their emancipation, their political independence and their sovereign equality among the nations.

Ben-Gurion read out Israel's Declaration of Independence which began with the words, "the Land of Israel was the birthplace of the Jewish people. Here they first attained to statehood, created cultural values of national and universal significance and gave to the world the eternal Book of Books."[49]

The Declaration was part poetry, part legalese. Part hopeful and romantic. Part defensive, still furiously trying to prove the legitimacy of a Jewish state in Palestine. In other words, flawlessly Jewish. It referred to Balfour, the Mandate and Resolution 181 (II). It spoke of "freedom, justice and peace as envisaged by the prophets of Israel". It beseeched the Jews of the world to "stand by them in the great struggle for the realization of the age-old dream – the redemption of Israel." It appealed to the Arabs within Israel "to preserve peace and participate in the upbuilding of the State on the basis of full and equal citizenship and due representation in all its provisional and permanent institutions." It extended also to its neighboring Arab states "an offer of peace and good neighborliness ... to establish bonds of cooperation and mutual help with the sovereign Jewish people settled in its own land."[50]

But of greatest importance was the declarative component itself. The document announced the national rebirth of the Jewish people: "By virtue of our natural and historic right and on the strength of the resolution of the United Nations General Assembly, [we] hereby declare the establishment of a Jewish State in Eretz-Israel (the land of Israel) to be known as the State of Israel."

On the same day, a letter was sent by the Jewish Agency to President Truman notifying him of the declaration of the State of Israel in accordance with Resolution 181 (II) and requesting that the United States "recognize and welcome Israel into the community of nations."[51] The same day President Truman issued a statement that the "United States recognizes the provisional government as the de facto authority of the new State of Israel."[52] The words "State of Israel" appeared handwritten over the struck out words "Jewish state", reflecting the late hour in which the new Jewish state was named. The Soviet Union would go one better than US de facto recognition and extend full legal recognition of the State of Israel on 17 May.

David Ben-Gurion reads the Declaration of Independence
(Government Press Office, Israel, Creative Commons).

WAR

But the period was not one of revelry and euphoria. As independence was declared the civil war that had commenced upon the adoption of the partition resolution, gave way to a full-scale military invasion of the new Jewish state by the armed forces of the neighboring Arab countries. Just three years after the end of the Holocaust era, a fresh sense of existential dread descended on the nation of Israel.

It was total war. The Israeli home-front was inescapably absorbed in every aspect of the conflict, frenetically following news reports of Egyptian air-raids over Tel Aviv, of Iraqi troop movements across the River Jordan, of advancing Egyptian boots in the south, and Syrian forces descending from the Golan Heights in the north towards Jewish villages in the Galilee. Meanwhile, in mixed Arab-Jewish cities like Jerusalem, Haifa and Jaffa, neighbor now feared neighbor and what the rap on the door could bring.

The author Devorah Nosovitsky described those days as living under a "grief regime" as news of the war dead fell upon household after household.[53]

5682 Israelis died in that war, amounting to 1% of the total population of the new state. Of the dead, 1162 were civilians and 362 were women.[54] But Israel repelled the invading forces and the new state survived.

With the invasion of Israel came the death of the Partition Plan, the end of diplomacy and low-scale violence, replaced by a campaign to thwart Zionism through overwhelming force. The mortal threat to world Jewry, which Zionism was created to cure, now hung over the State of Israel.

Israel emerged from the war with more territory than the Partition Plan had offered, while the chaos of the war resulted in a population exchange that would forever transform the Middle-East. Some 700,000 Arabs fleeing the fighting were displaced from the territory that had become Israel, and settled in neighboring Arab states or in Arab-held parts of the former mandate territory, where they would remain, often encamped, unintegrated, and in some cases subject to institutional discrimination by their fellow Arabs, until the present day.

Meanwhile, the vanquished Arab states expelled their Jewish communities which swelled the Jewish population of Israel. Between 1948 and 1952, Israel absorbed more than 710,000 Jewish migrants, almost half of those came from the Islamic world.[55] The sworn enemies of Israel had in effect become Zionist recruiters, forcing their ancient Jewish communities to resettle in Israel. This gave the new Jewish state the healthy Jewish majority that the Zionist leaders and the framers of the Paris Peace Conference and the British Mandate had always understood to be essential to the viability of a Jewish national home.

In the concluding observations of his history of the 1948 War, the historian Benny Morris observed the new reality that had set in in the Middle East:

> The Jewish state had arisen at the heart of the Muslim Arab world – and that world could not abide it. Peace treaties may eventually have been signed by Egypt and Jordan; but the Arab world – the man in the street, the intellectual in his perch, the soldier in his dugout – refused to recognize or accept what had come to pass. It was a cosmic injustice. And there would be plenty of Arabs; by habit accustomed to think in the long term and egged on by the ever-aggrieved Palestinians, who would never acquiesce in the new Middle East order. Whether 1948 was a passing fancy or has permanently etched the region remains to be seen.[56]

For decades, the Jews had vacillated between mainstream Zionist theory which sought a patch of earth the Jews could call their own, and revisionism which read international promises strictly and clung to original territorial demands. They agonized over migration quotas and debated the minimum number of Jewish arrivals they would be willing to abide. They gave speeches on the merits or pitfalls of partition that delved into the very essence of what Zionism meant and what Jewish statehood required. The Arabs meanwhile had been rigidly consistent in their position. No Jewish State, no Jewish migrants and no Jewish land acquisitions. And no resolutions of the United Nations or even a failed war would soon change that.

The decades that followed were conditioned wholly by these attitudes. The Jews of Palestine, now "Israelis", applied their opposing political, philosophical and cultural perspectives to every challenge and every opportunity.

In 1967, an extraordinary Israeli defensive campaign ousted the belligerent Arab armies in only six days and led to the capture of the Old City of Jerusalem including the site of the Jewish temples that Roman emperors thought the Jews would long forget, and the former Jewish heartland where Abraham was buried and the Maccabees led their hilltop rearguard. The area has come to be known as the "West Bank", for its geographic relationship to the River Jordan. Israel had also captured the old Philistine stronghold of Gaza and the Sinai Peninsula from the Egyptians and the Golan Heights from Syria.

But with this spellbinding conquest, Zionism and the State of Israel faced an almighty conundrum. Did security necessitate the permanent holding of these lands or could they be traded for offers of peace and recognition? Was it better to relinquish the ancient Jewish heartland captured in a defensive war, or hold the lands and remain imbedded with the millions of Arabs who live there? Could the partition principle still be rescued in some form and the Arabs in the West Bank granted autonomy or full statehood? Could the Arabs ever come to terms with a Jewish state in Palestine and finally live alongside the Jews in peace or was the legacy of al-Husseini irreversible?

Israelis debate these issues to this day. The Arabs again faced no such angst. At the conclusion of the 1967 war, at an emergency meeting of the Arab League in Khartoum, Sudan, the Arab world codified its relationship with Israel with three new 'no's' – no

Jewish state, no Jewish migration and no Jewish land purchases became "no peace, no recognition and no negotiations with Israel."

The state of war thus became permanent. A fresh invasion on multiple fronts was mounted in 1973 on Yom Kippur, the Jewish holy day of atonement. While Israel held the territories it had gained in 1967, the war bruised the Jewish state and shattered any semblance of invincibility that had arisen in the heady days of 1967.

Terrorism in essence replaced the pogrom as an ordinary condition of Jewish life. 38 civilians, including 13 children were killed when a passenger bus was hijacked on Israel's coastal highway in 1978. Thirty more were killed when a suicide bomber detonated inside a function center in Netanya in 2002 as Jews sat down to observe the Passover feast. 21 young Israelis, most of them teenagers, were ripped to pieces by a bomb laced with nails and ball-bearings detonated outside the Dolphinarium nightclub in Tel Aviv in 2001. Israeli athletes were tortured, castrated and executed at the Munich Olympic Games in 1972.

REHABILITATION

But the history of Zionism following the return to Jewish autonomous political development was also punctuated by striking achievements that would have surpassed even the utopian aspirations of the founders of the movement.

Predominant amongst these was the forging of peace with Arab neighbor states, including the historic Treaty of Peace between Egypt and Israel in 1979, which returned the Sinai Peninsula to

Egypt after its capture by Israel in the 1967 War, in exchange for peace and full diplomatic recognition in a formula known as "land for peace", as called for by United Nations Security Council Resolution 242.[57] Israel also signed a peace treaty with Jordan in 1994 and the Oslo Accords with the representatives of the Arab Palestinians in 1993, which presented a vision of mutual recognition, peace and economic union and a still unfulfilled pathway to a final end to the conflict. These treaties were achieved through a combination of Israel strength, which had demonstrated the futility of endless war against it, and the courageous pursuit of peace with the most bitter of enemies.

The ingathering of the Jewish exiles and the offering of sanctuary to vulnerable Jewish communities remains perhaps the defining achievement of the modern Jewish state. The eventual absorption of some 586,000 of the 820,000 Jews expelled from the Middle East and North-Africa, the rapid ingathering of roughly one million Jews from the former Soviet Union in the decade following its collapse and the daring rescue missions to repatriate threatened Jews in Yemen[58] and Ethiopia reflected the practical fulfilment of the Zionist promise and showed the curative and redemptive powers of Jewish statehood.

Alongside the conventional military prowess of the Jewish state that had seen the ragged Jewish militias mature into the most formidable fighting force in the region, Israel had developed a powerful counter-intelligence apparatus that was central to the preservation of the state. This saw the rehabilitation of the Jewish people from a nation of scattered communities incapable of acting as a single unit even to defend itself, to one that would strike with precision and force against all enemies.

Following the murder of Israeli athletes in Munich, Israel launched Operation Wrath of God, an intelligence mission spanning decades tasked with locating and killing the Palestinian terrorists. When Israeli intelligence caught wind of Iran supplying Palestinian militants in Gaza with weapons via Sudan, the Israeli air force conducted covert strikes on the weapons convoys and the munitions plants.[59] Nuclear reactors in Syria and Iraq disappeared with near nonchalance under Israeli fighter jets.

The trial of Adolf Eichmann in Jerusalem in 1961 transformed Jewish self-image once more. But now the Jew stood as accuser, the pointed finger of Israeli prosecutor Gideon Hausner demanding justice on behalf of "six million accusers".[60] Eichmann, who had been present during the adoption of the Final Solution at Wannsee and was the chief administrator of the process of mass deportation to the death camps, had been unceremoniously plucked from his Argentinian villa by Israeli agents and transported to Jerusalem. Now he pathetically twitched in a glass cage in the court-room, standing before the judges of Israel.

The legendary commando raid on an airfield in Entebbe, Uganda, overwhelmed the Palestinian terrorists who had hijacked an Air France liner en route from Tel Aviv, resulting in the liberation of the hostages, and the neutralization of the hijackers and much of the air-force of Idi Amin, the Ugandan despot who gave shelter to the terrorists. The raid projected Jewish strength, heroism and self-reliance like never before.

This was a new Israel, a new Jewish people, born of ancient traditions, hardened by bitter experience, with the pride of a people who had worked the land and defended it. A people no longer willing to plead with its oppressors.

Now Jewish intellect and education were being applied not only to meeting the urgent military needs of the state, but to doing something innovative, novel, useful that would be worthy of the grandeur of the Zionist project and the sacrifices of those who brought it into being.

In pre-state Israel it had been through land reclamation, soil enrichment, irrigation and other agricultural innovations. The same spirit was then applied to turning Israel into a cutting-edge marvel of biomedicine, information technology, engineering.

In *Start-Up Nation – the Story of Israel's Economic Miracl*e, the entrepreneur Erel Margalit explains the imperative to innovate as a new wave of Zionist creativity:

> You're not just trading in goods, or you're not just a finance person. You are doing something for humanity. The new pioneering Zionist narrative is about creating things.[61]

In truth, the Zionist narrative was always about creating things but now that "insatiable need to tinker, invent, and challenge,"[62] was being applied not merely to the up-building of a state for the Jews, but for advancements that have transformed human existence, from delivery of new medical treatments to computer processors and space stations.

Perhaps the most marvelous innovation of all has been the revival, adaptation and expansion of the Hebrew language by Eliezer Ben-Yehuda. Ben-Yehuda had little by way of Herzl's magnetism or Weizmann's charm. By all accounts he was a cantankerous recluse. But genius comes in various forms. Ben-Yehuda took a language that had come into virtual disuse save as a language of prayer, that had been succeeded by a bevy of language and dialects spoken by Jews across the world, and made it into the official, vernacular tongue to give common identity and common purpose to the ingathered exiles.

The language, one immersed in Jewish history, and indigenous to the lands which the Jews once again possessed, became central to the unifying mission of Zionism and to the forging of a new identity for the Jewish people, at once ancient and brand new.

Egyptian President Anwar Sadat and Israeli Prime Minister Menachem Begin acknowledge applause during a Joint Session of Congress in which President Jimmy Carter announced the results of the Camp David Accords (Warren K. Leffler, Public Domain).

An Israeli soldier helps new immigrants from Ethiopia arriving in Israel. (Government Press Office, Israel).

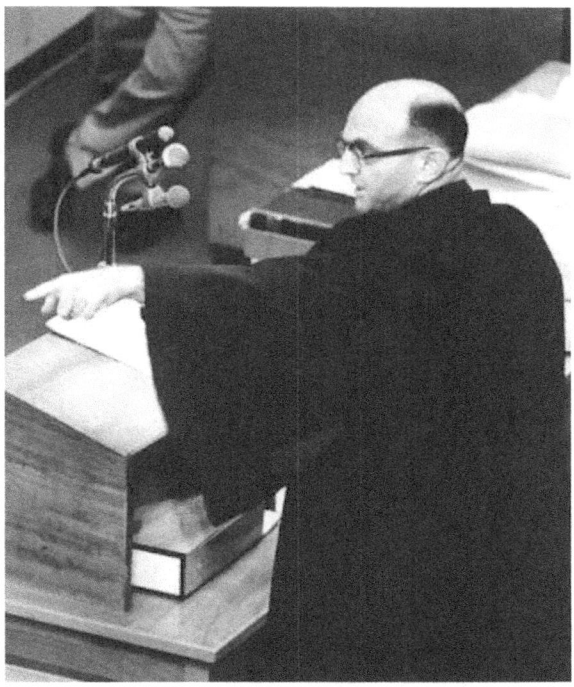

Gideon Hausner, the prosecutor at the trial of Adolf Eichmann delivers his opening statement, Jerusalem, 1961 (Courtesy of Yad Vashem).

10

ANTI-ZIONISM

EARLY ANTI-ZIONISM

Anti-Zionism can be understood as the attempt to thwart the objectives of Zionism, being the establishment of a national home for the Jewish people in Palestine. Zionism has always had its enemies, ranging from antisemites repelled by any movement to secure Jewish rights, to politicians and diplomats fearful of Arab antagonism, and some Jews themselves who held firmly to the path of assimilation and viewed Zionism as fanciful or disruptive.

The question of support for or opposition to Zionism began very much as an internal Jewish debate. Within more integrated Jewish communities in liberal-democratic societies, the emancipation of the Jews through full legal and civil rights was seen as the antidote to antisemitism. The French author Anatole Leroy-Beaulieu observed of the French Jews in 1894: "They have found [a homeland], by the rivers of the West, and are not at all desirous of changing it for the deserted banks of the Jordan."[1] Leroy-Beaulieu saw a people clamoring for equality as Frenchmen rather than longing for a return to Zion.

In the United States, Gustavus Poznanski, the spiritual leader of the rebuilt Kahal Kadosh Beth Elohim synagogue, in Charleston, South Carolina declared, "This synagogue is our temple, this city our Jerusalem, this happy land our Palestine, and as our fathers defended with their lives that temple, that city, and that land, so will their sons defend this temple, this city, and this land."[2] Poznanski spoke of a people who had happily accepted their condition of exile and had found their salvation not in a national return but in the melting pot of America.

In Britain, Edwin Montagu, who had been elected to the British Parliament and later served as Secretary of State for India and Minister of Munitions, viewed with alarm the growing support for Zionism in the British Government, and urged the British cabinet to reject Zionism in the months before the Balfour Declaration. He called the Jewish liberation movement a "mischievous political creed," and one he viewed as a pursuit for persecuted Russian Jews.[3]

Montagu, who had ascended to near enough the summit of British power, considered the emancipation of the Jews or a national home for the Jews, wholly unnecessary. Furthermore, he feared the impact that Zionism would have on his position in British society. Should the Jews be granted a national home in Palestine, he surmised, "Jews will hereafter be treated as foreigners in every country but Palestine."[4]

Equally strident in his opposition to Zionism was Sir Isaac Isaacs, the Jewish Australian who had the distinction of not only serving as Chief Justice of the Australian High Court and as a Member of Parliament, but was the first Australian-born Governor-General, or representative of the Monarch in Australia.

Like Montagu, Isaacs had achieved immense privilege within the framework of the liberal-democratic society of which he was a part. The very conception of a Jewish nationality would raise the specter of dual loyalties, Isaac feared. Rejecting the sympathies of Australian Jews for Zionism, Isaacs asserted: "Our simple duty is to our King and country in this hour of trial."[5]

Indeed, Leon Pinsker, whose writings were fundamental to the ascent of Zionism, had himself earlier advocated assimilation as the cure for antisemitism, and had done so in a country far less liberal or tolerant than America or Australia.

There can be little doubt of the bona fides of Jewish anti-Zionism in the years before the creation of the State of Israel. The hard-won advances in Jewish civil rights on the European continent, and the periods of intermittent calm in Russia, seemed to suggest that the pursuit of a place of refuge for the Jews was a far-fetched and unnecessary expedition.

Foremost in the minds of Jewish anti-Zionists was a concern that any movement that acknowledged the distinction between Jews and Gentiles, rather than emphasizing a commonality, would unwind the steady gains in civil rights and imperil Jews rather than liberate them.

It was for this reason that the German Socialist theorist, Karl Kautsky had called Zionism "a spoke in the wheel of progress."[6] Similarly, the Jewish human rights organization, the Alliance Israélite Universelle, feared that a "Jewish separatist movement could alienate the sympathies of their fellow citizens,"[7] concerns also variously expressed by Montagu and Isaacs, among others.

LATER ANTI-ZIONISM

But the events of the 1940s ended any serious contemplation over the correctness of Zionism. The Holocaust shattered the illusion that the Jews had no need for a place of refuge or that they could reliably hope to preserve their traditions, or even their lives in a world without a Jewish national home. Herzl had learned from the Dreyfus Affair that under even slight distress, systems of laws, proclaimed rights, and norms of human behavior, would be jettisoned and old hatreds, long nourished would surge through society's cracks like noxious weeds. Now, in the wake of the near annihilation of the Jews, to question the necessity of a Jewish state which could offer refuge to its scattered diaspora and protect the surviving Jews from further disaster, was a mockingly ludicrous position. But with the passage of time, this position would be gradually eroded by those either indifferent to the Holocaust or who found its lessons too historic or too remote to weigh on their political sensibilities.

If the Holocaust pushed anti-Zionism into intellectual irrelevance, the establishment of the State of Israel in May 1948, which represented the practical completion of Zionism, ensured that anti-Zionism ceased to be a tenable moral position. No longer the opposition to a movement or an idea, anti-Zionism now stood for the opposition to the continuing existence of the State of Israel. In other words, anti-Zionism now meant support for the destruction of a sovereign state.

As such, the cause of anti-Zionism was deserted by those genuinely concerned with alleviating Jewish suffering and preserving Jewish human and national rights. In the place of anti-Zionist assimilationist Jews like Isaacs and Montagu, and various special interests, there emerged a coalition of groups and actors, bitterly opposed to one another on all manner of things, but united completely in their desire to topple the state of the Jews.

The most lethal source of anti-Zionism of course continued to emanate from the Arab states, who upon failing in their initial attempt to thwart Zionism through threats and use of armed force, vowed openly to embark on future rounds of war in the not too distant future. Their new tone was one of militaristic bravado and a call for pan-Arabic conquest. Hafez al-Assad, who ruled Syria before the ascent of his son Bashar, declared on the eve of the 1967 War with Israel: "Strike the enemy's settlements, turn them into dust, pave the Arab roads with the skulls of Jews … We are determined to saturate this earth with blood and to throw you into the sea."[8]

Al-Husseini, whose political Islam sought to internationalize the Arab-Jewish conflict and turn anti-Zionism into an Islamic creed, would be succeeded in this regard by the Iranian regime following the Islamic Revolution in 1979. The old Grand Mufti of Jerusalem had held the Jews to be "blood-suckers"[9] with whom there could never be peace or accommodation. In 2012, the Iranian Supreme Leader, referred to Jewish statehood as a "cancerous tumor in the heart of the Islamic world",[10] in familiar language invoking both the threat to the body of Islam posed by Jewish national self-determination and the apparent need to violently excise the Jews.

Following the creation and survival of Israel, Jewish anti-Zionism, once led by eminent assimilationist Jews who cared deeply for the future of their people, became the domain of marginal figures in the Jewish diaspora. It would now be difficult to identify a single mainstream Jewish organization or representative body that is not institutionally committed to the security and survival of the State of Israel, though of course matters of Israeli government policy are as much a source of robust debate within Jewish communities outside Israel as they are within Israel itself.

Jewish Anti-Zionism is now characterized not by intellectual rigor and sincerity but by garish public displays of opposition with a distinctly anti-establishment flavor. Its sources are typically activists of the hard-left and minor factions of ultra-Orthodox Judaism, who oppose Zionism for its secular origins. A small Hassidic sub-sect, the Neturei Karta, has even taken to courting the Iranian regime to demonstrate the sincerity of their desire to see the obliteration of the Jewish state.[11]

The academic Shlomo Sand had become a darling of the anti-Zionist movement for seeking to undermine the premise of a Jewish national return by arguing that contemporary Jews bear no ethnic connection to those exiled from the Jewish province in ancient times. In a subsequent work titled, "How I Stopped Being a Jew", Sand spoke of his desire to no longer "be catalogued as a Jew."[12] In a similar vein, a group of Australian activists published a declaration purporting to renounce their right to migrate to Israel based on their Jewish ancestry.[13]

As Israel came to attain a central place of pride and Jewish identity both for Israelis and for the Jews who continue to live outside the Jewish state, public opposition to the existence of Israel has come to represent a form of "converting-out" of being Jewish. It serves as a repudiation of Jewish particularity in a way that is more complete and more ostentatious than quietly lapsing in one's religious practices. This is in sharp contrast with pre-

Israel anti-Zionist Jews, whose commitment to the Jewish people could not be faulted.

Alongside Arab/Islamic anti-Zionism, and small sects of anti-Zionist Jews, the political left has emerged as the other dominant force opposed to the continuing existence of a national home for the Jewish people.

It was not always so. We have seen that the one-time patron of the political left, the Soviet Union had been the first nation to offer legal recognition to the State of Israel, which followed the remarks by Andrei Gromyko at the United Nations, in which he deemed the denial of a Jewish state in Palestine to be "unjustifiable".[14]

In 1943, a leading Soviet diplomat gave a visiting Jewish delegation what became the conventional explanation for why the USSR decided to reverse its previous policy and support Zionism:

> Back in the twenties, we could not but consider Zionism as an agency of British imperialism. And we were bound to treat you accordingly. Now, however, the whole situation has changed. Not only do Britain and Zionism seem to be at a constant variance, but our outlook, too, has undergone a serious evolution. Should Soviet Russia be interested in the future in the Middle East, it would be obvious that the advanced and progressive Jews of Palestine hold out much more promise for us than the backward Arabs controlled by feudal cliques of kings and effendis.[15]

The Soviets had looked to the ruptured state of Zionist-British relations following the White Paper; they had observed the socialist-inspired communal farms and agricultural feats of the Jewish pioneers; they had noted the Russian roots of many of the Zionist founding fathers, and they saw potential allies.

In 1944, the British Labour Party adopted a position on Zionism, so extreme in its support of Jewish aspirations and so derisive of the Arabs that Ben-Gurion felt compelled to intervene, pointing out that the Zionists themselves had not been consulted in the drafting and that Jewish settlement of the land must not be detrimental to the Arabs.[16]

Left-wing support for Zionism peaked with the founding of Israel and the attempted military conquest of this infant state by far greater forces. Israel's refusal to succumb was positively awe-inspiring to adherents of political movements predicated on defeating mighty foes and toppling structures of power. As chronicled by Philip Mendes in his study of Zionism and the political left, "all international communist parties supported partition and the creation of a Jewish State."[17] The US Communist Party called Israel "an organic part of the world struggle for peace and democracy", while the French Communists viewed the Jewish fighters as the comrades of resistance fighters throughout the world.[18]

But as Israel charted its own course, emerged from its wars economically and militarily superior to the Arabs, and became more ambitious and assertive in how it conducted its security affairs, the support of the Soviet Union and of the international left entered a sharp decline, followed by a complete reversal.

Ben-Gurion had assured the US Ambassador that while "Israel welcomes Russian support in the UN, it will not tolerate Russian domination." "Israel", Ben-Gurion noted, is "western in its orientation, its people are democratic, and realize that only through the co-operation and support of the US can they become strong and remain free."[19] Israel's "western orientation" became clear to the Soviet Union following its joining Britain and France in the Suez Campaign in 1956 to liberate a key maritime route linking Asia to Europe amidst threats to nationalize the canal by Egypt's President Gamal Abdel Nasser, a key Soviet ally.

The Soviets viewed the campaign against Egypt as a direct threat to its strategic power in the Middle East. The outrage was heightened by the broader context of the escalation, which came amidst uprisings against Soviet authority in Poland and Hungary, which the Soviets viewed as being fueled by Western agitation. This all contributed to send Moscow into a state of foaming apoplexy, resulting in threats to deploy nuclear weapons against the British and French and to annihilate Israel entirely.[20]

The Soviet Union had already cut diplomatic relations with Israel in February 1953, only weeks before the death of Stalin and after a period of rapid escalation of state antisemitism, culminating in the notorious "Doctors' Plot", in which Jewish doctors in the Soviet Union were accused of plotting to poison Party officials.

Soviet support for Zionism had generally been more about strategic aims and Cold War calculations than upholding the justness of a Jewish home. As Herzl had learned in his dealings with antisemites in Berlin, Istanbul and Moscow, while interests may momentarily align between a Zionist and an antisemite, a national rights movement cannot rely upon the fleeting graces of those who despise the nation itself.

The hope created by Gromyko's gallant words and by senior Soviet diplomats raising their glasses to toast "to the future of the Jewish State"[21] spectacularly unraveled into nothing. The Soviet Union now stood as the arch-enemy of Zionism, arming the Arab armies on Israel's frontiers, artfully jostling them into provoking Israel into military action, and ensuring through its unrivalled capacity for propaganda, that the concept of Zionism and anyone who dared to support it, would soon be drenched in infamy.

US Ambassador to the United Nations, Daniel Moynihan
(Marion S Trikosko, Public Domain).

Soviet Ambassador to the United Nations Andrei Gromyko.
(RIA Novosti, Creative Commons).

RED TERROR

Once the policy of the Soviet Union towards Israel became one of abject hostility, the state media was saturated with anti-Zionist propaganda, which simply repurposed the antisemitic canards of old, that had a deep resonance with a public steeped in hostility and derision towards the Jews.

In 1963, an antisemitic tract titled "Judaism without Embellishment", authored by a Ukrainian Nazi sympathizer, Trofim Kichko, was published by the Ukrainian Academy of Sciences. The themes of the book were tediously familiar – a global Jewish conspiracy, a world under threat from Jewish manipulations of world finance, and Jews pulling the strings of capitalism and imperialism. It was a latter-day Secret Protocols of the Elders of Zion and it would be a harbinger of a literary barrage to come aimed at resurrecting old passions and turning the gullible peoples of the world against the Jews and their nation-state.

Titles began appearing such as "Caution: Zionism!", "Fascism under the Blue Star," "Invasion without Arms," "Zionism's Secret Weapon", "A Hotbed of Zionism and Aggression". Kichko himself would return with updated publications titled, "Judaism and Zionism" and "Zionism – Enemy of the People".[22] Soviet newspapers were again publishing cartoons of bloated, hook-nosed Jewish bankers and all-consuming serpents embossed with the Star of David.

Anti-Zionism had become virtually indistinguishable from antisemitism. What was once a legitimate, though ultimately disproven political theory, that sought to enlarge Jewish rights through assimilation, had become the tool for assaulting the basic humanity of the Jewish people.

As the British political theorist Alan Johnson observed, "what 'the Jew' once was in older antisemitism – uniquely malevolent, full of blood lust, all-controlling, the hidden hand, tricky, always acting in bad faith, the obstacle to a better, purer, more spiritual world, uniquely deserving of punishment, and so on – the Jewish state now is..."[23] The target of antisemitism had merely shifted from one form of Jewish self-identification to another – from Jewish rituals, Jewish faith and the Jewish community, to the Jewish state.

The images and publications would go well beyond the Soviet reader. Through Soviet satellites in Europe, South America and the Middle East, and through communist chapters and socialist publications throughout the world, these ideas would reach a global audience, eventually nestling in far-left circles in the West, including political parties, human rights organizations, militant trade unions, and of course, campuses.

The propaganda was highly compelling – vivid, dramatic, clear, consistent and urgent. It would be based in long-established themes of Jewish bloodthirstiness, greed, corruption, manipulation and cunning. It would contend that the very existence of a Jewish homeland was not only a plot of imperialism, but a mortal danger to the peace of the world.

It was what Hitler called the "big lie" – the use of dramatically overblown fiction to deceive the public. Hitler, the supreme propagandist observed that the bigger the lie the more believable it was: "It would never come into people's heads to fabricate colossal untruths, and they would not believe that others could have the impudence to distort the truth so infamously ..."[24]

The big lies would soon find their way into the most influential forums in the world. When a sub-commission of the United Nations was tasked with drafting a convention on the "elimination of all forms of racial discrimination", the proceedings focused on contemporary forms of racism notably, apartheid, neo-Nazism and antisemitism. The Soviets however, who viewed the reference to antisemitism as a direct rebuke to their anti-Jewish measures, parried and served up an amendment that "was almost a joke", even to the Soviet delegation itself.

The amendment inserted Zionism into the listed forms of racism, alongside apartheid and Nazism.[25] According to sources close to the deliberations, the Soviets understood "full well that the idea that Zionism is racism is an indefensible position",[26] yet they floated it anyway, in part to turn the US-led initiative into farce, and in part perhaps, to see how far a "big lie", could go.

Ultimately, the Convention was adopted with neither antisemitism nor Zionism referred to – the ploy had worked.[27] But the seed had been planted. In June 1975, the UN staged the World Conference on Women in Mexico City, which concluded with the adoption of the Declaration of Mexico on the Equality of Women and their Contribution to Development and Peace. The Declaration listed Zionism alongside racism and apartheid as an evil destined for elimination.[28]

A few months later, on 10 November 1975, when the General Assembly of the United Nations convened in New York, Resolution 3379 on the "elimination of all forms of racial discrimination" was put before the nations of the world. Expressly referring to the Declaration already adopted in Mexico City, Resolution 3379 noted the earlier designation of Zionism as having a "racist structure" and constituting a "threat to world peace and security" and determined that "Zionism is a form of racism and discrimination." The Resolution passed overwhelmingly, 72 for, 35 against, 32 abstaining.[29]

Less than three decades after recommending partition to create a Jewish homeland in fulfilment of the very ideals and hopes of Zionism, a majority of the nations of the world had determined that same Zionism, the national liberation movement of the Jewish people, was a form of racism.

The propaganda that the peace-loving peoples of the world were victims of the Jews, the blatant inversions of truth that had been used to justify mass slaughter, had become internationally-sanctioned positions.

Addressing the General Assembly the following day, Israel's Ambassador to the United Nations, Chaim Herzog said:

> For us the Jewish people, this Resolution based on falsehood, hatred and arrogance is devoid of any moral or legal value. For us the Jewish people, this is no more than a piece of paper and we shall treat it as such.

Upon concluding his words, Herzog tore a copy of the Resolution in half before leaving the podium.[30]

On the same day as the Resolution was passed, the US Ambassador to the United Nations Patrick Moynihan issued a press release rejecting the Resolution in terms that seethed with an outrage and a fury not only at what the Resolution meant for its target, but for the very concept of truth.

> There will be time enough to contemplate the harm this act will have done the United Nations. Historians will do that for us, and it is sufficient for the moment only to note one foreboding fact.

> A great evil has been loosed upon the world. The abomination of antisemitism has been given the appearance of international sanction. The General Assembly today grants symbolic amnesty -- and more – to the murderers of the six million European Jews.[31]

Moynihan declared the proposition that Zionism is a form of racism to be "a lie ... but a lie which the United Nations has now declared to be a truth." He continued, calling it a "political lie of a variety well known to the twentieth century, and scarcely exceeded in all that annal of untruth and outrage."

Considering the impact that the Resolution would have beyond the corridors of the United Nations, Moynihan charged: "The harm will arise first because it will strip from racism the precise and abhorrent meaning that it still precariously holds today. How will the peoples of the world feel about racism, and about the need to struggle against it, when they are told that it is an idea so broad as to include the Jewish national liberation movement?"[32]

Moynihan understood the full implications of such a lie being laundered into respectability by the United Nations. Such a brazen assault on truth conducted in a forum of immense moral authority and prestige was a threat to the international system itself. Indeed, it is arguable that despite repealing Resolution 3379 in 1991, the credibility of the United Nations has never fully recovered.

The impact of the Resolution on the course of what had become a full-blown attack on the State of Israel in international forums by targeting Zionism as the foundational movement on which the state was built, was profound.

The proposition that Zionism is a form of racism, now "declared to be truth" by the United Nations, could be used to purge mainstream Jewish voices from popular movements and civil society organizations.

In 1977, at least 17 student unions in Britain debated motions along the lines of Resolution 3379. York, Salford, Warwick and Lancaster went further, passing motions to expel their Jewish societies "on the grounds that they are Zionist and therefore racist".[33]

The Resolution gave an impetus, an urgency and a credibility to those intent on stirring anti-Zionist feeling in the public domain. The concept of denying platforms to fascist and white supremacist speakers on university campuses was now being applied to stifle mainstream voices who expressed support for the State of Israel.[34]

Moynihan had observed this logic in his statement following the passage of Resolution 3379. An earlier UN resolution had, at the instigation of the Soviet Union, viewed "racism to be merely a form of Nazism". It followed that if racism is merely a form of Nazism and Zionism is a form of racism, then Zionism is a form of Nazism.[35]

On this basis, anti-Zionist students could harass Zionist speakers and be seen as taking a noble stand against a form of Nazism. This double-speak was applied much later by the organizers of the annual Chicago Dyke March, a pride parade, whose organizers had prevented Zionists from marching in 2017, on the basis that Zionism was an "inherently white-supremacist ideology."[36] A similar attempt was made to exclude Zionist women from a series of feminist marches in the United States, on the grounds that Zionism is incompatible with feminism.[37]

Giving international sanction to the "Zionism is racism" lie, had precisely the impact on truth that Moynihan foresaw. It had become possible, even plausible, to explicitly associate Zionism, a movement for Jewish liberation, with Nazism, a movement for Jewish destruction. This proposition also had origins in Soviet anti-Zionist literature, consistent with linking Zionism with popular conceptions of evil.

As has been discussed, it was then resurrected and peddled to modern audiences by Ken Livingstone, a socialist, who served as Labour mayor of London between 2000 and 2008. In a series of interviews in 2016 and 2017, Livingstone claimed that there was "real collaboration" between the Nazis and the Jews, and that Hitler "… was supporting Zionism before he went made and ended up killing six million Jews."[38] The theme of Jews becoming the new Nazis, a double blow that associates Zionism with supreme evil and mocks the victims of the Holocaust by equating them with their murderers, has become a mainstay of anti-Zionist discourse.

With the emergence of Israel as a military power, and with the state's increasing effectiveness in disrupting and limiting the lethality and scale of terrorist attacks, anti-Zionism undertook a tactical realignment.

Of course, statements about the looming destruction of Israel still abound. "Israel won't exist in 25 years",[39] the Iranian Supreme Leader declared in 2015. But the anti-Zionist campaign is now less about achieving total victory in scenes of blazing Jewish cities and marching Arab armies, and more about bringing about the eventual collapse of a Jewish sovereign presence in the Middle East through a process of political isolation that would result in the abandonment or forced reconstruction of the state's character as the Jewish homeland.

This aim was articulated by Abu Iyad, the head of security

services for the Palestine Liberation Organization, in 1972. Abu Iyad acknowledged that Israel had "staying power". But he calculated that this was precariously founded on the national morale of its people that was being kept high by Western governments who assured Israel's continued existence. "If one could succeed in changing public opinion in the Western world," Abu Iyad believed, "then the overthrow of Zionism would just be a matter of time."[40]

The public opinion to which Abu Iyad referred is that Israel is legitimate, that its existence is just and necessary and that the Jews have a right to a national home. This had been established over a period of decades by the advocates of Zionism and had been accepted by the international community. It had been sanctified with the blood of the slain European Jews and Israeli soldiers and civilians alike. But public opinions can change, even ones as elemental as the belief that a people should have a national home in some part of the lands from where they came. The anti-Zionists were now exhibiting a strategic patience.

Following another ill-fated United Nations conference, this time in Durban, South Africa, from 2001, the boycott, divestment and sanctions (BDS) campaign emerged as the popular movement to target organs of government and civil society to shift public opinion about Israel and Zionism's legitimacy. Modelled on anti-war and anti-apartheid movements, BDS evokes the imagery of resistance, appropriates the language of human rights and international law, and makes a direct appeal to the spirit of rebellion by casting Israel and its supporters as all-powerful and uniquely evil and those who oppose it as enlightened and morally pure.

BDS is often misunderstood as seeking to apply economic leverage on Israel, coercing it into making concessions to Palestinian nationalist demands. More correctly, BDS seeks to recruit to the cause of anti-Zionism by offering an illusory, seemingly peaceful alternative to war and terror for those uncomfortable with Israeli government policies and drawn to the romance of guerilla and popular resistance movements. It claims to offer a solution to the Israeli-Palestinian impasse, one rooted in justice, and thereby gains an entry point into the debate on Israel. This in turn enables its adherents to saturate audiences with familiar accusations of Zionist racism, Nazism and other atrocities as a way of eroding support for Israel. Insofar as the framers of the campaign have articulated their goal as "... the defeat of Zionist Israel"[41] and "... to bring down the state of Israel",[41] BDS can be seen as a modern tactic of the broader, longer anti-Zionist campaign and wholly incompatible with human rights and international law.

Ultimately, if the vestiges of Soviet anti-Zionist/antisemitic propaganda, the "big lies", could take hold in meaningful institutions in society, if the opponents of Zionism could advance, through brazen repetition, the view of Israel as a state founded on a principle akin to racism and Nazism, surely "public opinion in the Western world" could indeed be changed. And with that, as Abu Iyad assured, the "overthrow of Zionism would be just a matter of time".

To students and observers of Jewish history it will be of little surprise to see how fragile the modern State of Israel may be, despite its impressive military and economic achievements. If Zionism can be branded racist in the same chamber that had a mere 28 years earlier overwhelmingly affirmed Zionism by approving the creation of a Jewish state in Palestine; if the Jews who survived Nazism could be branded Nazis themselves even in a time when the victims, perpetrators and liberators of the Nazi death camps and killing fields remain alive to bear witness, then nothing can be taken for granted.

It is the lot of the Jewish people to exist in a state of perpetual unease, to lurch from calamity to disaster, to fight ceaselessly to win fundamental rights automatically extended to others, only for those rights to be trampled or withdrawn at a later time with no hint of irony and no regard for history. And if the right to practice their faith according to their customs, the right to be treated equally with non-Jewish citizens, the right to live without fear of expulsion or forced conversion, the right even to live, can all be trounced, who is to say that the right to a national home will not similarly be withdrawn?

Zionism, we have seen, is a remarkable story of an ancient people who by all rational examination should not be here today, certainly not as Jews practicing customs and traditions almost indistinguishable from those of their ancient forebears. It is the story of that people's survival through a sheer will to endure and to remain. It is the story of individuals possessed with a rare genius and extraordinary ability to lead and to inspire, that turned a shapeless yearning to go home from a bland epithet recited in prayer or laconically uttered at the festive table, into a political program of grand scale that could be implemented within the norms and systems of the day. It is a story colored as much by its villains as by its heroes – death certificates on white papers, Nazi executioners and Grand Muftis played as much a part in the course of Zionist history as did Herzl, Weizmann and Ben-Gurion.

And it is a story that continues with no end in sight, as Jews and Israelis debate, as Lincoln did for America at Gettysburg, what their national project truly means and the enemies of Zionism, steel themselves for a war they have yet to concede.

NOTES

1 Zion

1. Michael G Hasel. "Israel in the Merneptah Stela." *Bulletin of the American Schools of Oriental Research.* 296 (1994): 45-61, p.45.

2. Ibid.

3. "The Tel Dan Inscription: The First Historical Evidence of King David from the Bible". *Biblical Archaeology Society.* May 2, 2019.

4. Donald Redford. *Egypt, Canaan and Israel in Ancient Times.* (Princeton, Princeton University Press, 1992). p.310.

5. Paul Johnson. *A History of the Jews.* (Weidenfeld and Nicolson, London, 1987). p.63, note 186.

6. Flavius Josephus. *Jewish Antiquities.* Translated by William Whiston, (Wordsworth Editions, Hertfordshire, 2006). p.430.

7. Paul Johnson, Op. Cit. p.83.

8. Book of Jeremiah (29:6).

9. Book of Jeremiah (29:6).

10. Book of Jeremiah (29:14).

11. Simon Sebag Montefiore. *Jerusalem: The Biography.* (Orion Publishing, London, 2011). p.123.

12. Flavius Josephus, *The Destruction of the Jews.* Translated by G. A. Williamson, (Folio Society, London, 1971). p.216.

13. Paul Johnson, Op. Cit. p.143.

14. Flavius Josephus, Op. Cit. p.213.

15. Rabbi Micah Peltz, "Why I Still Fast on Tisha B'Av", August 8, 2011, *Haaretz.*

2 Thunder

1. The French National Assembly, "Debate on the Eligibility of Jews for Citizenship" (December 23, 1789). In *The Jew in the Modern World.* Edited by P.R. Mendes-Flohr and J. Reinharz (Oxford University Press, New York, 1995). p.115.

2. Ibid.

3   Bernard Lewis. *The Jews of Islam*. (Princeton University Press, Princeton, 1987). pp.44-45.

4   The French National Assembly. Op. Cit. p.116.

5   A. Malamat, H. Tadmor, M. Stern, S. Safrai and H. H. Ben-Sasson (editor). *A History of the Jewish People*. (Harvard University Press, Cambridge, 1966). p.656.

6   Anatoly Kuznetsov. *Babi Yar. A Document in the Form of a Novel*. Translated by David Floyd. (Farrar, Straus and Giroux, London, 1970). p.106.

7   George Orwell. *Down and Out in Paris and London*. (Text Publishing, Melbourne, 2016), p.48.

8   Paul Johnson. Op. Cit. p.365.

9   Leon Pinsker. *Auto-Emancipation: An Appeal to His People by a Russian Jew*. 1881. (Translated from the original Russian and Yiddish to English and accessible online at Jewish Virtual Library).

3 J' Accuse!

1   Louis Begley. *Why the Dreyfus Affair Matters*. (Yale University Press, New Haven, 2009). Published in extract form in *The Washington Post*, October 11, 2009.

2   Paul Johnson, Op. Cit. p.380.

3   Ibid. p.392, note 169.

4   Theodor Herzl. *The Jewish State*, (1896). Translated from the German by Sylvie D'Avigdor and published in 1946 by the American Zionist Emergency Council. Accessible online at Jewish Virtual Library.

5   Daniel Polisar. "The Most Politically Significant Meeting of Any Group of Jews in the Last 1,800 Years - The story of Theodor Herzl and the First Zionist Congress, convened 120 years ago on this date". *Mosaic Magazine*, August 23, 2017.

6   Edmond Fleg. *Why I am a Jew*. (Bloch Publishing Company, New York, 1945). p.37.

7   Saul Bellow. *To Jerusalem and Back – A Personal Account*. (Avon Books, New York, 1976).

8   Lawrence J. Epstein. *The Dream of Zion: The Story of the First Zionist Congress*. (Rowman & Littlefield Publishers, Lanham, 2016), p.105.

NOTES

4 London

1. Simon Sebag Montefiore. *Jerusalem: The Biography*. (Orion, London, 2011) p.377.

2. Ibid. p.376.

3. Theodor Herzl. "Address to Fourth Zionist Congress, August 13, 1900, London". Translated from the German by Nellie Straus. Federation of American Zionists. 1917.

4. Cecil Bloom. "Samuel Montagu and Zionism". *Jewish Historical Studies*. 34 (1994): 17-41. p.34.

5. Ibid. p.31.

6. Gabriel Sheffer. "A Practical Man's Vision of Utopia". *Haaretz*. October 26, 2001.

7. Ibid.

8. "Jewish Massacre Denounced". *The New York Times*, April 28, 1903.

9. Philip Ernest Schoenberg. "The American Reaction to the Kishinev Pogrom of 1903". *American Jewish Historical Quarterly*. 63, 3 (1974): 262-83. p.268.

10. Ibid.

11. Matt Lebovic. "How a small pogrom in Russia changed the course of history". *Times of Israel*. April 9, 2018.

12. S. N. Dubnow. *History of the Jews in Russia and Poland from the Earliest Times Until the Present Day*. Translated by I. Friedlander. Vol.2 (The Jewish Publication Society of America, Philadelphia, 1920) p.128.

13. H.N. Bialik. "The City of Slaughter" in *Complete Poetic Works of Hayyim Nahman Bialik*. Edited by Israel Efros (The Histadruth Ivrith of America, New York, 1948): pp.129-43

5 Chemistry

1. Yuval Azoulay. "Jacobus Street, Corner of Oblivion". *Haaretz*. April 1, 2009.

2. Paul Johnson, Op. Cit. p.399.

3. Ibid.

4. Ben Halpern. "Review of 'Chaim Weizmann' by Isaiah Berlin (1959). *Commentary Magazine*. May 1959.

5. Jehuda Reinharz. "Science in the Service of Politics: The Case of Chaim Weizmann during the First World War". *The English Historical Review*. 100, 396 (1985): 572-603. p.583.

6. Ibid. p.582.

7. Ibid. p.600.

8. Chaim Weizmann. "The Guardian and the Balfour Declaration, Azriel Bermant". *Fathom Journal.* Summer 2017.

9. Reinharz, Op.Cit. p.601.

10. Ibid.

11. Ibid. p.573.

12. Josh Glancy. "Chaim Weizmann and how the Balfour Declaration was made in Manchester". *Jewish Chronicle.* November 1, 2012.

13. Sir Isaiah Berlin. "The Biographical Facts". In Meyer W. Weisgal and Joel Carmichael, Editors. *Chaim Weizmann; A Biography of Several Hands.* (Weidenfeld and Nicolson, London, 1962) p.36. Quoted in Chaim Weizmann and the Balfour Declaration: "A Unique Act of World Moral Conscience". Joel Fishman. Jerusalem Center for Public Affairs. February 27, 2017.

6 Balfour's Note

1. Chaim Weizmann. *Trial and Error – The Autobiography of Chaim Weizmann.* (Greenwood Publishing Group, London, 1972) p.262.

2. Text of Balfour Declaration, November 2, 1917. Accessed online through The Rothschild Archives.

3. Stephen Oryszczuk. "Lord Rothschild discusses cousin's crucial role in 'miracle' Balfour Declaration". *Times of Israel.* February 8, 2017.

4. Ruth Lapidoth. "Is the Balfour Declaration a Legally Binding Document?" *Jewish Political Studies Review.* 28, 1/2 (2017). p.43.

5. Stephen Oryszczuk, Op. Cit.

6. Century Ireland historical database, RTE. Entry on Gallipoli and Zion Mule Corps.

7. John Henry Patterson. *With the Zionists In Gallipoli.* (George H. Doran Company, New York, 1916) p.208.

8. "The Lion-Killer Who Became an Israeli Hero". *British Broadcasting Corporation Magazine.* November 30, 2014.

9. Paul Heinrichs. "Simpson's Donkey? What About Zlotnik's Mules?". *The Age.* April 23, 2006.

10. Correspondence by French Foreign Minister Jules Cambon to Nahum Sokolow, dated June 4, 1917. Quoted in "The Historical Significance of the Balfour Declaration", Ambassador Dore Gold. Jerusalem Center for Public Affairs. October 31, 2017.

11. "Woodrow Wilson's Fourteen Points, President Wilson's Message to Congress" January 8, 1918. Records of the United States Senate. Record Group 46; Records of the United States Senate. National Archives.

NOTES

12. Ibid.

13. Wilson Papers, File VI, No. 618. August 31, 1918. Quoted in Selig Adler. "The Palestine Question in the Wilson Era". *Jewish Social Studies* 10:4 (October, 1948). pp.303-334.

14. The Churchill White Paper, June 3, 1922. Accessed through the digital document archive of the United Nations, Question of Palestine.

15. Report of a Committee Set Up to Consider Certain Correspondence Between Sir Henry McMahon (His Majesty's High Commissioner in Egypt) and The Sharif Of Mecca in 1915 and 1916. Presented by the Secretary of State for the Colonies to Parliament by Command of His Majesty, March 16, 1939. Accessed through the digital document archive of the United Nations, Question of Palestine.

16. Selig Adler. "The Palestine Question in the Wilson Era". *Jewish Social Studies*. 10:4 (October, 1948). pp.303-334, note 66.

17. Isaiah Friedman. *Palestine, A Twice-promised Land?: The British, the Arabs & Zionism, 1915–1920*. (Transaction Publishers, New Brunswick, 2000) p.171.

18. J. C. Hurewitz (Editor). *Middle East & North Africa in World Politics*. Second edition (Book 2). (Yale University Press, New Haven, 1979) p.136.

19. Ibid.

20. The Covenant of the League of Nations. Accessed through the digital archive of the US Department of State. Office of the Historian. Papers Relating to the Foreign Relations of the United States. The Paris Peace Conference, 1919, Volume XIII.

21. Preamble to the Covenant of the League of Nations. Accessed through the digital archive of the US Department of State. Office of the Historian. Papers Relating to the Foreign Relations of the United States, The Paris Peace Conference, 1919, Volume XIII.

22. Woodrow Wilson's Fourteen Points. Ibid.

23. Martin Gilbert. *Israel, A History*. (Black Swan, London, 1998) p.42.

24. League of Nations Mandate for Palestine, August 12, 1922. Accessed through the digital document archive of the United Nations, Question of Palestine.

25. J. C. Hurewitz (Editor). *Middle East & North Africa in World Politics*. Second edition (Book 2). (Yale University Press, New Haven, 1979) p.136.

26. Yoram Ettinger. "Who were the 1948 Arab Refugees?". *The Algemeiner*. June, 6, 2016.

27. Ibid.

28. The Churchill White Paper, June 3, 1922. Accessed through the digital document archive of the United Nations. Question of Palestine.

29. Ibid.

30. Ibid.

31. Ibid.

32. The Churchill White Paper. Op. Cit.

33. Mark Twain. *The Innocents Abroad, 1869*. (web edition published by eBooks@ Adelaide), Chapter 56.

34. The Churchill White Paper. Op. Cit.

35. Nadav G. Shelef. "From 'Both Banks of the Jordan' to the 'Whole Land of Israel': Ideological Change in Revisionist Zionism". *Israel Studies*. 9:1 (2004): 125-48. p.127.

36. Chaim Weizmann. *Trial and Error – The Autobiography of Chaim Weizmann*. (Greenwood Publishing Group, London, 1972) p.262.

7 Clash

1. J. C. Hurewitz (Editor). *Middle East & North Africa in World Politics*. Second edition (Book 2). (Yale University Press, New Haven, 1979) p.136.

2. Ibid.

3. League of Nations Mandate for Palestine, August 12, 1922. Accessed through the digital document archive of the United Nations, Question of Palestine.

4. The Covenant of the League of Nations. Article 22. Accessed through the digital archive of the US Department of State. Office of the Historian,.Papers Relating to the Foreign Relations of the United States.The Paris Peace Conference, 1919. Volume XIII.

5. Martin Gilbert. *Israel, A History*. (Black Swan, London, 1998) p.51.

6. Nadav Shragai. "The Al-Aksa is in Danger, Libel: The History of a Lie", *Jerusalem Center for Public Affairs*. 2012, Chapter 3. Note 3.

7. Alex Winder. "The 'Western Wall' Riots of 1929: Religious Boundaries and Communal Violence". *Journal of Palestine Studies*. 42:1 (2012): 6-23. p.18.

8. Ibid. p.15.

9. Ibid.

10. Ibid. p.19.

11. David B. Green. "Hebron Massacre Begins, With a Big Push from the Mufti". *Haaretz*. August ,23, 2016.

12. Martin Gilbert. Op. Cit. p.69.

NOTES

13. Ibid. p.65.

14. Ibid. p.61.

15. Ricki Hollander. "Anti-Jewish Violence in Pre-State Palestine/1929 Massacres". Camera.org. August 23, 2009.

16. Pierre Van Paassen. *Days of our years.* (Hillman-Curl, London, 1940).

17. Martin Gilbert, Op. Cit. p.61.

18. W. Shaw et al. "Report of the Commission on the Palestine Disturbances of August 1929 (Shaw Commission), March 1930 [Excerpts]". In Abdul Hadi, M., Editor. *Documents on Palestine, Volume I Until 1947.* (Passia, Jerusalem, 2007) pp.155-158.

19. Martin Gilbert, Op. Cit. p.66.

20. David B. Green. "Hebron Massacre Begins, With a Big Push from the Mufti". *Haaretz.* August 23, 2016.

21. W. Peel et al. (1937), "Report of the Palestine Royal Commission", accessed through the digital document archive of the United Nations, Question of Palestine.

22. Benny Morris. "Revisiting the Palestinian Exodus of 1948". In: Eugene L. Rogan and Avi Shlaim, Editors. *The War for Palestine,* (Cambridge University Press; Cambridge, 2007) pp.40-41.

23. Peel Commission Report, Findings and Recommendations of the Royal Commission, excerpts (July 1937), Royal Institute of International Affairs, Great Britain and Palestine, 1915-1945, Information Paper No. 20, Oxford University Press, 1947. 155-9, republished by Center for Israel Education, in preamble by Ken Stein.

24. M. MacDonald. "British White Paper of 1939. Accessed through the digital archive of the Yale University. The Avalon Project – documents in law, history and diplomacy.

25. Ibid.

26. Martin Gilbert, Op. Cit. p.90.

27. Walter Laqueur and Barry Rubin, Editors. *The Israel-Arab Reader.* (Penguin Books, New York, 2001).

28. Michael J. Cohen, "Appeasement in the Middle East: The British White Paper on Palestine, May 1939." *The Historical Journal.* 16,3 (1973): 571-96, p. 587.

29. Ibid. p.591, note 72.

8 Inferno

1. Leon Pinsker. *Auto-Emancipation: An Appeal to His People by a Russian Jew.* 1881. (Translated from the original Russian and Yiddish to English and accessible online at Jewish Virtual Library)..

2. Leviticus 26:3-27:34..

3. Raul Hilberg. *The Destruction of the European Jews.* (Holmes & Meier, London 1985) pp.19-20.

4. Steve Boggan. "The anti-Jewish lie that refuses to die". *The Times of London.* March, 2, 2005.

5. Quoted in the pamphlet by Dr Karl Bergmeister. "The Jewish World Conspiracy. The Protocols of the Elders of Zion before the Court in Berne". Erfurt, 1938.

6. Raul Hilberg. Op. Cit. p.14.

7. Ibid. p.16.

8. Yehuda Bauer. *The Holocaust in Historical Perspectives.* (ANU Press, Canberra, 1970) p.9.

9. Anatoly Kuznetsov. *Babi Yar. A Document in the Form of a Novel.* Translated by David Floyd. (Farrar, Straus and Giroux, London, 1970).

10. Raul Hilberg. Op. Cit. p.338.

11. Doyle Rice. "15,000 murders a day: August-October 1942 were the Holocaust's deadliest months." *USA Today.* January 2, 2019.

12. Martin Gilbert. *Atlas of the Holocaust.* (NWilliam Morrow and Company, New York, 1993) pp.242-244.

13. Efraim Zuroff. *Occupation, Nazi-Hunter – the continuing search for the perpetrators of the Holocaust.* (KTAV Publishing House, Brooklyn, 1994), p. xv.

14. Marvin Kalb. "Refugee crises and the sad legacy of the 1938 Evian conference". Brookings Institute. September 23, 2015.

15. "Summary of the outcomes from the Evian Conference and its ramifications for German-Jewish policy given by the Nazi intelligence and security body in July 1938". Submitted to SS Gruppenfuehrer Heydrich. Yad Vashem Archive, 0.51/OSO/37 Berlin. July 29, 1938. Accessed through Facing History and Ourselves.

16. Mike Lanchin. "SS St Louis: The ship of Jewish refugees nobody wanted. BBC World Service. May 13, 2014.

17. Marcus Dysch. "Operation Embarrass? You bet: Britain's secret war on the Jews". *The Jewish Chronicle.* September 21, 2010.

18. United States Holocaust Memorial Museum. Holocaust Encyclopedia, entry titled: "The Kielce Pogrom: A Blood Libel Massacre of Holocaust Survivors."

NOTES

19. István Deák, Jan T. Gross, Tony Judt, Editors. *The Politics of Retribution in Europe: World War II and Its Aftermath* (Princeton University Press, Princeton, 2009). p.112.

20. Comments by Professor Jan Grabowski in an interview with Colin Perkel. "Canadian Holocaust scholar says he's a target of Polish 'hate' campaign". *The Canadian Press.* June 20, 2017.

21. Jeffrey Herf. "Haj Amin Al-Husseini, the Nazis and the Holocaust: The Origins, Nature and Aftereffects of Collaboration." *Jewish Political Studies Review.* 26.3/4 (2014): 13-37. p.16.

22. Ibid.

23. Tom Segev. "Netanyahu's fairytale about Hitler and the mufti is the last thing we need". *The Guardian.* October 22, 2015.

24. Central Intelligence Agency, Biographic Sketch No. 60. Haj Amin al-Husayni, the Mufti of Jerusalem, April 24, 1951. Declassified and released by the CIA in 2006. Accessed through CIA digital archives.

25. Conversation of July 2, 1942, lunch at the Wolfsschanze: Henry Picker, ed., Hitlers Tischgespräche in Führerhauptquartier: Hitler, wie er werklich war (Stuttgart: Seewald, 1977), 403-404, quoted in Joel Fishman, The Historical Problem of Haj Amin al-Husseini, "Grand Mufti of Jerusalem", Jerusalem Center for Public Affairs, August 22, 2016.

26. Full official record: What the mufti said to Hitler, *Times of Israel,* October 21, 2015.

27. Jeffrey Herf, Op. Cit. p.26.

28. Ibid. p.29.

29. Telegram from SS Commander Heinrich Himmler to Amin al-Husseini, November 2, 1943. Released by the National Library of Israel on March 29, 2017.

30. United States Holocaust Memorial Museum, Holocaust Encyclopedia, entry titled, Hajj Amin Al-Husayni: Wartime Propagandist.

31. Joel Fishman. "The Historical Problem of Haj Amin al-Husseini, 'Grand Mufti of Jerusalem'". *Jerusalem Center for Public Affairs.* August 22, 2016.

32. Sara Bender. *The Jews of Białystok During World War II and the Holocaust.* (Brandeis University Press, Waltham, 2008). p.272.

33. Video of remarks by Ken Livingstone, published by the Guardian under the title: "What Ken Livingstone said about Hitler and Zionism – video". April 5, 2017.

34. Toi Staff. "Full official record: What the mufti said to Hitler". *Times of Israel.* October 21, 2015.

35 Extracts from Mein Kampf by Adolf Hitler, published digitally by Yad Vashem, the World Holocaust Remembrance Center.

36 David Ben Gurion. *Rebirth and Destiny of Israel.* (Philosophical Library New York, 1954) p.41.

37 Peter Novick. *The Holocaust in American Life* (Mariner Books, New York, 2000). pp.68-69.

38 Shlomo Nakdimon. "How Elie Wiesel the Journalist Saw Israel". *Haaretz*, July 9, 2016.

39 Gershon Greenberg. "German Displaced Persons Camps (1945-1948): Orthodox Jewish Responses to the Holocaust." *Historical Reflections / Réflexions Historiques.* 39.2 (2013): 71-95. p.72.

9 Israel

1 Letter from King Abdul Aziz Ibn Saud to President Roosevelt, copy transmitted to the United States Department of State by the Minister in Egypt in his des patch, No. 1034, May 11, 1943; received May 25, accessed through the digital archive of the Office of the Historian, US Department of State, Foreign Relations of The United States: Diplomatic Papers, 1943, the Near East And Africa, Volume IV.

2 Jeffrey Herf. "Haj Amin Al-Husseini, the Nazis and the Holocaust: The Origins, Nature and Aftereffects of Collaboration.". *Jewish Political Studies Review.* 26.3/4 (2014): 13-37. p.31, note 57.

3 Report of Earl G. Harrison – mission to Europe to inquire into the condition and needs of those among the displaced persons in the liberated countries of Western Europe and the SHAEF area of Germany – with particular reference to the Jewish refugees – who may possibly be stateless or non-repatriable, "The Harrison Report", sent to President Truman, accessed through digital archives of Dwight D, Eisenhower Presidential Library.

4 Ibid.

5 Françoise Ouzan."Rebuilding Jewish identities in Displaced Persons Camps in Germany". *Bulletin du Centre de recherche français à Jérusalem.* Marc, 30, 2004. p.107.

6 Ibid. p.106, note 14.

7 Raphael Langham. "The Bevin Enigma: What Motivated Ernest Bevin's Opposition to the Establishment of a Jewish State in Palestine." *Jewish Historical Studies.* 44 (2012): 165-78. p.173

8 Ibid.

9 Ibid.

10 Third Report by Mrs M. Warburg, Foehrenwald Hospital, November 15, 1945

NOTES

CZA S26/1303, quoted in Françoise Ouzan, "Rebuilding Jewish identities in Displaced Persons Camps in Germany", Bulletin du Centre de recherche français à Jérusalem, March, 30, 2004. p.107.

[11] Raphael Langham. Op. Cit. p.175.

[12] Martin Gilbert. Op. Cit. p. 121.

[13] Quoted in *Blockade: The Story of Jewish Immigration to Palestine 1933-1948* by Gerald Ziedenberg, (Author House, 2011), p.156.

[14] Zev Golan. "Jewish Assassins In Cairo". *The Jerusalem Post*. October 16, 2013.

[15] W. S. Churchill, House of Commons debate, Palestine (Terrorist Activities), November 17, 1944, accessed through digitized editions of Commons and Lords Hansard.

[16] Martin Gilbert. Op. Cit. p.118.

[17] Ibid.

[18] Colin Shindler."Opposing Partition: The Zionist Predicaments after the Shoah." *Israel Studies*. 14.2 (2009): 88-104. p.94.

[19] "Ben-Gurion Reveals Suggestion of North Vietnam's Communist Leader", Jewish Telegraphic Agency, *Daily News Bulletin*. November 8, 1966.

[20] Immigration into Palestine: Statement by President Truman, October 4, 1946, Department of State Bulletin of October 13, 1946, pp. 669-670, accessed through the digital archive of the Yale University, The Avalon Project – documents in law, history and diplomacy.

[21] Ritchie Ovendale. "The Palestine Policy of the British Labour Government 1947: The Decision to Withdraw". *International Affairs* (Oxford) 56, 1 (1980) 73-93. p.90.

[22] Greer Fay Cashman. "The King David Hotel Bombing: Letting The People Judge the Truth". *Jerusalem Post*. July 23, 2016.

[23] Paul Johnson. Op. Cit. p.521.

[24] Ernest Bevin, House of Commons debate, Palestine (Government Policy), February 25, 1947, accessed through digitized editions of Commons and Lords Hansard.

[25] Ibid.

[26] Ibid.

[27] Martin Kramer. "Why the 1947 UN Partition Resolution Must Be Celebrated". *Mosaic*. November 27, 2017.

[28] Testimony from Representatives of the Arab States – UN Special Committee on Palestine (UNSCOP) 38th meeting – Verbatim Record, Held at the Ministry of Foreign Affairs; Beirut, Lebanon, on Tuesday July 22, 1947, accessed through the

digital document archive of the United Nations, Question of Palestine.

[29] Peter Grose. "The Partition of Palestine 35 years ago". *The New York Times Magazine*. November 21, 1982.

[30] Rabbi Abba Hillel Silver address to Zionist General Council meeting in September 1947, quoted in "The 1947 UN Partition Plan," Britain Israel Communications and Research Centre, November 2017.

[31] Speech by David Ben-Gurion to the Elected Assembly of Palestine Jews, October 2, 1947, accessed through the digital archive of the Israeli Ministry of Foreign Affairs.

[32] Ibid.

[33] Letter from David Ben-Gurion to his wife, quoted in "The 1947 UN Partition Plan", Britain Israel Communications and Research Centre, November 2017.

[34] Speech by David Ben-Gurion to the Elected Assembly of Palestine Jews, October 2, 1947, accessed through the digital archive of the Israeli Ministry of Foreign Affairs.

[35] Anita Shapira. *Ben-Gurion, Father of Modern Israel* (Yale University Press, New Haven, 2014). p. 156.

[36] Peter Grose. "The Partition of Palestine 35 years ago". *The New York Times Magazine*. November 21, 1982.

[37] Paul Johnson. Op. Cit. p.525.

[38] Peter Grose. Op. Cit.

[39] Speech by Andrei Gromyko to the Seventy-Seventh Plenary Meeting of the United Nations General Assembly. New York. May 14, 1947.

[40] Peter Grose. "The Partition of Palestine 35 years ago". *The New York Times Magazine*. November 21, 1982.

[41] Statements by representatives of Arab states to United Nations General Assembly in response to the adoption of Resolution 181 (II), accessed through the digital archive of the Israeli Ministry of Foreign Affairs.

[42] Sam Lipski. "UN Partition Resolution – a day we should celebrate". *Australian Jewish News*. December 1, 2017.

[43] Amoz Oz. *A Tale of Love and Darkness*, (Mariner Books, Brooklyn, 2005).

[44] Moshe Dayan. *Story of My Life*. (William Morrow and Company, New York, 1976).

[45] Libby Galvin. "On this day: The Hadassah medical convoy massacre", *Jewish Chronicle*. April 13, 2011.

[46] Speech by David Ben-Gurion to the Elected Assembly of Palestine Jews,

NOTES

October 2, 1947, accessed through the digital archive of the Israeli Ministry of Foreign Affairs.

47 Elon Gilad. "Why is Israel called Israel?. *Haaretz*. April 20, 2015.

48 Martin Gilbert. Op. Cit. p.187.

49 The Declaration of Independence of the State of Israel, May 14, 1948, accessed through the digital database of the Israel State Archives.

50 Ibid.

51 Letter by Eliahu Epstein to Harry S. Truman regarding recognition of Israel, May 14, 1948, found in Truman Papers, Official File. 204-D: Jewish State, 1948-49, accessed through the digital archives of the Harry S. Truman Presidential Library.

52 Press Release about Recognition of Israel Charles G. Ross, Alphabetical File Handwriting of the President Harry S. Truman Presidential Library Independence, MO, accessed through the digital archives of the US National Archives.

53 Devorah Nosovitsky. 'Mothers at the Home Front', quoted in Naor, Moshe. "Israel's 1948 War of Independence as a Total War." *Journal of Contemporary History*. 43.2 (2008): 241-57. p.255.

54 Moshe Naor. "Israel's 1948 War of Independence as a Total War." *Journal of Contemporary History*. 43.2 (2008): 241-57. p.254.

55 Immigrants to Israel, 1948-1952. Accessed through the digital archives of the Israel State Archives.

56 Benny Morris. *1948: A History of the First Arab-Israeli War*, (Yale University Press, New Haven, 2009). p.420.

57 United Nations Security Council Resolution 242 (1967), November 22, 1967, also known as "land for peace" resolution, accessed through the digital document archive of the United Nations, Question of Palestine.

58 Isabel Kershner. "19 Yemeni Jews Arrive in Israel, Ending Secret Rescue Operation". *The New York Times*. March 21, 2016.

59 "Sudan blames Israel for Khartoum arms factory blast," British Broadcasting Corporation. October 24, 2012.

60 Opening address of Gideon Hausner in the trial of Adolf Eichmann, April 11, 1961. Jerusalem, published electronically by the Museum of the Jewish People.

61 Dan Senor and Saul Singer. *Start-Up Nation, The Story of Israel's Economic Miracle* (Hachette Book Group, London, 2011). p.228.

62 Ibid.

10 Anti-Zionism

1. Robert S. Wistrich.. "Zionism and Its Jewish 'Assimilationist' Critics (1897-1948)." *Jewish Social Studies,* New Series, 4.2. (1998): 59-111, p. 63.

2. Michael A. Meyer. *Response to Modernity: A History of the Reform Movement* (Wayne State University Press, Detroit, 1995). pp.233-234.

3. Ibid.

4. Memorandum of Edwin Montagu on the Anti-Semitism of the Present (British) Government - Submitted to the British Cabinet, August 1917. Accessible online at Jewish Virtual Library.

5. Zelman Cowen. "Isaacs, Sir Isaac Alfred (1855–1948)'. *Australian Dictionary of Biography* (Melbourne University Press, Melbourne, 1983).

6. Karl Kautsky. "Are the Jews a Race?". Quoted in Philip Mendes. *Jews and the Left.* (Palgrave Macmillan, London, 2014) p.97.

7. H. Nahum to Paris, November 2, 1909 and copy of letter from J. Bigart to H. Nahum, November 26, 1909 (Alliance Israelite Archives, Turquie XXX), quoted in Wistrich, Robert S. "Zionism and Its Jewish "Assimilationist" Critics (1897-1948)." *Jewish Social Studies.* New Series, 4.2 (1998): 59-111. p.66.

8. John Podhoretz. "Are We Drinking the Hezbollah Kool-Aid?". *National Review.* August 18, 2006.

9. Jeffrey Herf. "Haj Amin Al-Husseini, the Nazis and the Holocaust: The Origins, Nature and Aftereffects of Collaboration." *Jewish Political Studies Review.*26.3/4 (2014): 13-37. p.16.

10. Greg Tepper. "Israel a 'cancerous tumor' and Middle East's biggest problem, Iranian supreme leader says". *Times of Israel.* August 19, 2012.

11. "Neturei Karta: Ahmadinejad wants peace". *Yedioth Ahronoth.* September 25, 2007.

12. Shlomo Sand. "Shlomo Sand: 'I wish to resign and cease considering myself a Jew'". *The Guardian.* October 11, 2014.

13. "Petition against the Right of Return to Israel on behalf of Australian Jews". February 2010. Published on website of Australians for Palestine.

14. Discussion of the report of the First Committee on the establishment of a special committee on Palestine (documents A/307 and A/307/Corr. 1), Seventy-Seventh Plenary Meeting, held in the General Assembly Hall of the United Nations, New York, May 14, 1947, accessed through the digital document archive of the United Nations, Question of Palestine.

15. Arnold Krammer. "Soviet Motives in the Partition of Palestine, 1947-48." *Journal of Palestine Studies.* 2.2 (1973): 102-19. p.109.

NOTES

16   Cecil Bloom. "The British Labour Party and Palestine, 1917-1948". *Jewish Historical Studies.* 36 (1999): 141-7. p.147.

17   Philip Mendes. "The Australian Left's Support for the Creation of the State of Israel, 1947-48." *Labour History.* 97 (2009): 137-48. p.139

18   Ibid.

19   James G. McDonald. "My Mission to Israel, 1948-1951" quoted in Arnold Krammer. "Soviet Motives in the Partition of Palestine, 1947-48." *Journal of Palestine Studies.* 2.2 (1973): 102-19. p.106.

20   O. M. Smolansky. "Moscow and the Suez Crisis, 1956: A Reappraisal." *Political Science Quarterly* .80.4 (1965): 581-605. p.589.

21   Arnold Krammer. "Soviet Motives in the Partition of Palestine, 1947-48." *Journal of Palestine Studies.* 2.2 (1973): 102-19. p.106.

22   Dave Davies. "Soviet Anti-Zionist Campaign". *Australian Left Review.* No. 76.

23   Alan Johnson. "Labour Party's anti-Semitism Inquiry Findings Show the Party Has Failed to Learn". *Haaretz.* July 1, 2016.

24   Quoted in Joel Fishman, "The Big Lie and the Media War Against Israel: From Inversion Of The Truth to Inversion of Reality." *Jewish Political Studies Review* 19, no. 1/2 (2007): 59-81, p 65.

25   Remarks by Dr. Meir Rosenne, former Consul of Israel at a World Zionist Organization Information Department, Seminar held at the US State Department in 1984, quoted in Joel Fishman (2011) "A Disaster of Another Kind": Zionism=Racism, It Beginning, and the War of Delegitimization against Israel", *Israel Journal of Foreign Affairs,* 5:3, 75-92, p. 77.

26   Ibid.

27   International Convention on the Elimination of All Forms of Racial Discrimination, adopted and opened for signature and ratification by General Assembly resolution 2106 (XX) of 21 December 1965, entry into force 4 January 1969, in accordance with Article 19. 246 Report of the World Conference of the International Women's Year, Mexico City, 19 June – 2 July 1975, accessed through the digital archive of the United Nations Women Watch project.

28   Ibid.

29   Resolution 3379 (XXX) on the elimination of all forms of racial discrimination, adopted by the General Assembly of the United Nations on November 10, 1975, accessed through the digital document archive of the United Nations, Question of Palestine.

30   Speech by Chaim Herzog, Ambassador of Israel to the United Nations, to the General Assembly of the United Nations. November 10, 1975.

31   Statement by Ambassador Daniel P. Moynihan, United States Representative to

the United Nations, in explanation of vote on the resolution equating Zionism with racism and racial discrimination. November 10, 1975. Accessed through the digital archives of the American Jewish Committee.

32 Ibid.

33 Dave Rich. "Hatred at the heart of the campus wars". *Jewish Chronicle.* November 2, 2015.

34 Sarah Ditum. "'No platform' was once reserved for violent fascists. Now it's being used to silence debate". *New Statesman America.* March 18, 2014.

35 Statement by Ambassador Daniel P. Moynihan. Op. Cit.

36 Kerry Cardoza. "Chicago Dyke March returns after clash last year became international news". *Chicago Reader.* June 13, 2018.

37 "Linda Sarsour: Zionism and Feminism Are Incompatible". Jewish Telegraphic Agency. March 15, 2017.

38 Video of remarks by Ken Livingstone, published by the Guardian under the title, "What Ken Livingstone said about Hitler and Zionism – video". April 5, 2017.

39 Eliott C. McLaughlin. "Iran's supreme leader: There will be no such thing as Israel in 25 years. CNN. September 11, 2015.

40 Quoted in E. W. Pless (pseudonym for Willi Pohl or Willi Voss) Geblendet: Aus den authentischen Papieren eines Terroristen (Zurich: Schweizer Verlagshaus, 1979), pp. 48- 50, extracted in "Antisemitism and anti-Zionism in West Germany in the 1970s: Lessons for Today", Martin Jander, *Fathom Journal*, Summer 2017.

41 Ronnie Kastrils speech at Israeli Apartheid Week event, 2009, published on website of "BDS Movement".

42 As'ad Abu Khalil. "A Critique of Norman Finkelstein on BDS", February 17, 2012.

APPENDIXES

THE BASEL PROGRAM

The first manifesto of the Zionist movement, the Basel Program was drafted by a committee of the first Zionist Congress led by Max Nordau, and unanimously adopted by the Congress on August 30, 1897. It set out the goals of the Zionist movement.

Zionism seeks to establish a home for the Jewish people in Palestine secured under public law.

The Congress contemplates the following means to the attainment of this end:

1. The promotion by appropriate means of the settlement in Palestine of Jewish farmers, artisans, and manufacturers.

2. The organization and uniting of the whole of the Jewish people by means of appropriate institutions, both local and international, in accordance with the laws of each country.

3. The strengthening and fostering of Jewish national sentiment and national consciousness.

4. Preparatory steps toward obtaining the consent of governments, where necessary, in order to reach the goals of Zionism.

THE DECLARATION OF INDEPENDENCE OF THE STATE OF ISRAEL

The land of Israel was the birthplace of the Jewish people. Here their spiritual, religious and national identity was formed. Here they achieved independence and created a culture of national and universal significance and gave to the world the eternal Book of Books.

After being forcibly exiled from their land, the Jewish people remained faithful to it in all the countries of their dispersion, never ceasing to pray and hope for their return and the restoration of their national freedom.

Impelled by this historic attachment, Jews strove in every successive generation to re-establish themselves in the land of their fathers and regain their statehood. In recent decades they returned in masses. They reclaimed the wilderness, revived their language, built cities and villages and established a vigorous and thriving community with its own economic and cultural life. They sought peace, but were always prepared to defend themselves. The brought the blessings of progress to all inhabitants of the country.

In the year 1897, the First Zionist Congress, inspired by Theodor Herzl's vision of a Jewish State, proclaimed the right of the Jewish people to national revival in their own country.

This right was acknowledged by the Balfour Declaration of November 2, 1917, and re-affirmed by the Mandate of the League of Nations, which gave explicit international recognition to the historic connection of the Jewish people with Palestine and their right to reconstitute their National Home.

The Nazi holocaust, which engulfed millions of Jews in Europe, proved anew the urgency of the re-establishment of the Jewish state, which would solve the problem of Jewish homelessness by opening the gates to all Jews and lifting the Jewish people to equality in the family of nations.

The survivors of the European catastrophe, as well as Jews from other lands, proclaiming their right to a life of dignity, freedom and labor, and undeterred by hazards, hardships and obstacles, have tried unceasingly to enter Palestine.

In the Second World War the Jewish people in Palestine made a full contribution in the struggle of the freedom-loving nations against the Nazi evil. The sacrifices of their soldiers and the efforts of their workers gained them title to rank with the peoples who founded the United Nations.

On November 29, 1947, the General Assembly of the United Nations adopted a Resolution for the establishment of an independent Jewish State in Palestine, and called upon the inhabitants of the country to take such steps as may be necessary on their part to put the plan into effect.

This recognition by the United Nations of the right of the Jewish people to establish their independent State may not be revoked. It is, moreover, the self-evident right of the Jewish people to be a nation, as all other nations, in its own sovereign State.

ACCORDINGLY, WE, the members of the National Council, representing the Jewish people in Palestine and the Zionist movement of the world, met together in solemn assembly today, the day of the termination of the British mandate for Palestine, by virtue of the natural and historic right of the Jewish and of the Resolution of the General Assembly of the United Nations,

HEREBY PROCLAIM the establishment of the Jewish State in Palestine, to be called **ISRAEL**.

WE HEREBY DECLARE that as from the termination of the Mandate at midnight, this night of the 14th and 15th May, 1948, and until the setting up of the duly elected bodies of the State in accordance with a Constitution, to be drawn up by a Constituent Assembly not later than the first day of October, 1948, the present National Council shall act as the provisional administration, shall constitute the Provisional Government of the State of Israel.

THE STATE OF ISRAEL will be open to the immigration of Jews from all countries of their dispersion; will promote the development of the country for the benefit of all its inhabitants; will be based on the precepts of liberty, justice and peace taught by the Hebrew Prophets; will uphold the full social and political equality of all its citizens, without distinction of race, creed or sex; will guarantee full freedom of conscience, worship, education and culture; will safeguard the sanctity and inviolability of the shrines and Holy Places of all religions; and will dedicate itself to the principles of the Charter of the United Nations.

THE STATE OF ISRAEL will be ready to cooperate with the organs and representatives of the United Nations in the implementation of the Resolution of the Assembly of November 29, 1947, and will take steps to bring about the Economic Union over the whole of Palestine.

We appeal to the United Nations to assist the Jewish people in the building of its State and to admit Israel into the family of nations.

In the midst of wanton aggression, we still call upon the Arab inhabitants of the State of Israel to return to the ways of peace and play their part in the development of the State, with full and equal citizenship and due representation in its bodies and institutions - provisional or permanent.

We offer peace and neighborliness to all the neighboring states and their peoples, and invite them to cooperate with the independent Hebrew nation for the common good of all.

Our call goes out to the Jewish people all over the world to rally to our side in the task of immigration and development and to stand by us in the great struggle for the fulfillment of the dream of generations - the redemption of Israel.

Placing our trust in the Rock of Israel, we set our hand to this Declaration, at this Session of the Provisional State Council, on the soil of the homeland, in the city of Tel Aviv, on this Sabbath eve, the fifth of Iyar, 5708, the fourteenth day of May, 1948.

Index

20th British Infantry Corps 82
4th Australian Light Horse Brigade 82
Abdullah 101
Abraham (The Patriarch) 187
Abu Iyad 211, 212
acetone (Weizmann's experiments with) 72, 73, 75, 76
Ad Hoc Committee on the Palestinian Question 172
Aelia Capitolina 27
Agnon, S.Y. 116
Ahuzat Bayit 67
Al Qibla newspaper 88
Al-Aqsa Mosque 20, 113
al-Assad, Hafez 199
al-Banna, Hassan 159
Alexander the Great 24
Alexander II (Tsar) 42
Alexander III (Tsar) 39
Alexander, Samuel 77
Alexandria 83, 101
al-Husseini, Haj Amin 109, 112, 13, 115, 116, 118, 145, 146, 147, 148, 149. 150, 151, 152, 154, 159, 180, 199
Alliance Israelite Universelle 197
Allied Powers 77, 92, 94, 96, 107
Altneuland (book by Theodor Herzl) 50

Amidah 29
Amin, Idi 190
Antiochus Epiphanes 24
Arab Higher Committee 160, 169, 178, 180
Arendt, Hannah 134
Ark of the Covenant 20
Ashkelon 18, 28
Assembly of Palestine Jews 171
Auschwitz-Birkenau Camp 136
Australia and New Zealand Army Corps (ANZACs) 83
Auto-emancipation (book by Leon Pinsker) 41, 42, 43
Babi Yar massacre 38
Babylon 21, 22, 23, 24, 25, 28, 54
Babylonian Exile 23
Babylonians 22, 31
Balfour Declaration 74, 75, 78, 79, 81, 82, 85, 86, 87, 88, 89, 90, 97, 99, 101, 102, 107, 1127, 114, 147, 148, 163, 168. 169, 179, 196
Balfour, Arthur James 60, 63, 74, 77, 79, 82
Bandera, Stepan 145
Basel Program 53, 55
Bauer, Yehuda 131
Beersheba 82

Beilis Affair 68
Bellow, Saul 53
Ben Shemen 66
Bergen-Belsen concentration camp 144, 154, 160
Belzec concentration camp 136
Ben-Gurion, David 118, 156, 163, 166, 167, 171, 172, 181, 182, 184, 202, 214
Ben-Yehuda, Eliezer 191
Berger, Gottlob 149
Berlin, Isaiah 70, 77
Bern 130
Bet-Tsuri, Eliahu 165
Bevin, Ernest 162, 163, 168, 169
Bialik, Hayim Nahman 62, 63, 92, 116,
Bialystock 149
Bishop of Clancy 33
Black Sabbath 166, 167
Bloody Sunday 63
Bludan Conference 118, 145
Bogdan Chmelnitsky 36, 125
Bogdanovca (massacre of Jews in) 135
Bosnia 149, 151
Boycotts, Divestment and Sanctions (BDS) campaign 212, 213
Brandeis, Louis D. 86
British Labour Party 201
British White Paper (1922) 161
British White Paper (1939) 161
Buber, Martin 106
Bucharest (massacre of Jews in) 135
Budapest (massacre of Jews in) 136
Bulgaria (treatment of Jews in) 145
Cambon, Jules 85
Cape Helles 83
Carlsbad (Zionist Congress meeting in) 99

Cattan, Henry 169
Central Intelligence Agency (CIA) 147, 225
Chamberlain, Neville 124
Chanukah 25, 29
Chelmno concentration camp 136
Chicago Dyke March 210
Christian Zionism 62
Churchill, Winston 14, 63, 72, 87, 98, 100
Coastal Highway massacre 188
Commentary on Zephaniah 28
Cooper Union 62
Cossack rebellion 36
Count of Clermont-Tonnerre 33
Croatia (treatment of Jews in) 149
Croatian Ustashe 145
Crusaders 129
Cyrus 22, 23
Czechoslovakia 123, 170
Damascus 108
Daniel Deronda (book by George Eliot) 60
Dardanelles 83, 84
David, King, 19, 20, 21
Dayan, Moshe 179, 180
de Hirsch, Baron Maurice 55
Deganya 66
Denmark (treatment of Jews in) 145
Die Welt newspaper 50
displaced persons camps 141, 160, 164, 168, 171
Doctors' Plot 203
Dolphinarium nightclub terror attack 188
Dome of the Rock 20

INDEX

Down and out in Paris and London (book by George Orwell) 38
Dreyfus Affair 45, 48, 50, 126, 198
Dreyfus, Captain Alfred 13, 45, 46, 47, 48
Dubnow, Shimon 140
East End (London) 59
Eban, Abba 175
Egypt 25, 83, 87, 113, 159, 186, 203
Eichmann, Adolf 134, 149, 157, 190, 193
Eichmann Trial 190
Einsatzgruppen 132
Einstein, Albert 106
Eliot, George 60
Entebbe (Israeli commando raid) 84, 190
École Militaire 46, 81
Esterhazy, Ferdinand Walsin 45, 46
Evatt, Herbert Vere ('Doc") 172
Evian Conference 140
Eytan, Walter 182
Faisal 88, 89, 101, 178
Fez (massacre of Jews in) 32, 53
Fifth Zionist Congress 66
Final Solution to the Jewish question 136, 147
First Aliyah 43
First Temple (see also Solomon's Temple) 20
First Zionist Congress 66
Five Books of Moses 25
Ford, Henry 130
Fourth Zionist Congress 53
France (treatment of Jews in) 32, 33, 35, 46, 49, 93, 96, 139, 140, 141, 190, 202
Franco-Prussian War 46

Frangie, Suleiman 169
Frankfurter, Felix 86
French National Assembly 32, 35
Freud, Sigmund 106
Gallipoli 83
Gaza 28, 82, 187, 190
George, David Lloyd 63, 73, 75, 76, 93
Germany (treatment of Jews in) 35, 57, 65, 69, 74, 89, 90, 123, 124, 141, 148, 152, 153, 154, 159, 168
Grabowski, Jan 145
Granada massacre 126
Grand Mufti of Jerusalem (see also "Haj Amin al-Husseini") 112, 145, 145, 149
Great War (See also World War I) 72, 74, 93, 102, 122
Greece 24, 25, 128
Gromyko, Andrei 173, 175, 201, 203, 204
Haavara (Transfer) Agreement 152, 154, 155
Hadassah Hospital (terror attack) 180
Hadrian 27, 28, 30, 40, 84
Haganah 164, 165, 166
Haifa 82, 95, 141, 185
Hakim, Eliahu 165
Hannover, Nathan 37
Harrison, Earl (see also "Harrison Report") 160, 168
Harrison Report 160
Hausner, Gideon 190, 193
Hebrew University 86, 106
Hebron 30, 110, 117, 157, 171
Hebron riots (see also "Western Wall riots") 111, 112, 113, 116, 164, 180
Hedera 43
Hejaz (Hashemite Kingdom of) 97

241

Hep-Hep pogrom 35
Herzl, Theodor 13, 14, 15, 39, 45, 48, 49, 50, 51, 52, 53, 54, 55, 56, 57, 58, 59, 60, 65, 66, 69, 70, 71, 77, 81, 138, 146, 166, 191, 198, 203, 214
Herzog, Chaim 208
Hilberg, Raul 128
Himmler, Heinrich 148, 149, 151
Hitler, Adolf 90, 123, 131, 141, 142, 147, 148, 152, 154, 155, 159, 206
Ho Chi Minh 166
Holocaust 14, 26, 36, 38, 125, 128, 131, 134, 142, 150, 155, 156, 157, 164, 167, 173, 184, 198
Holy of Holies 20
Hungarian Arrow Cross 145
Hungary (treatment of Jews in) 32, 203
Hussein ibn Ali 87, 97
Ibn Saud, King Abdul Aziz 159
Indian lancers 82
Iranian Supreme Leader 199, 211
Iraq 96, 101, 107, 178, 190
Irgun 164, 165, 166, 167, 180
Iron Age 18
Isaacs, Isaac 197, 198, 199
Israel's Declaration of Independence 182
Jabotinsky, Vladimir 15, 83, 84, 101, 102, 164
Jaffa 66, 67, 106, 185
Jedbawne (massacre of Jews in) 135
Jeremiah (Prophet) 23, 24, 73
Jerome 28, 29, 110
Jerusalem 13, 17, 19, 20, 21, 22, 23, 25, 27, 28, 29, 30, 54, 59, 66, 82, 86, 98, 108, 109, 110, 111, 112, 113, 117, 145, 149, 167, 170, 171, 172, 180, 181, 185, 187, 190, 193, 196, 199
Jewish Agency 115, 122, 152, 156, 165, 167, 183
Jewish Chronicle newspaper 49, 181
Jewish National Fund 66, 67, 146
Johnson, Alan 206
Joly, Maurice 130
Joseph II 32
Josephus 22, 26, 28
Judaism Without Embellishment (book by Trofim Kichko) 205
Judea 24, 26, 28, 77, 170, 181
Kaiser Wilhelm II 56
Kann, Jacobus 67
Kautsky, Karl 197
Khartoum Conference 187
kibbutz 66
Kichko, Trofim 205
Kielce (massacre of Jews in) 142
King David Hotel (bombing of) 167
Kingdom of Israel 19, 21, 22
Kingdom of Judah 21, 22
Kishinev pogrom 64, 116
Kristallnacht 39, 124
Kronstadt rebellion 63
Kuznetsov, Anatoli 133
Lapidoth, Ruth 80
Latvian Arajs Commando 145
League of Nations 91, 100, 102, 105, 106, 168, 169
League of Nations Covenant 91, 92, 96
League of Nations Mandate for Palestine 94, 96, 102, 114
Lebanon 96, 107
Lehi 164
Leroy-Beaulieu, Anatole 195
Lewis, Bernard 35
Livingstone, Ken 154, 211
Lord Moyne (assassination of) 165

INDEX

Lost tribes of Israel 22
Luther, Martin 139, 131
Maccabees 187
Maidanek concentration camp 136
Manchester Guardian newspaper 76
Margalit, Erel 191
Masada 27, 138
Matsui, Keishiro 93
May Laws 39
McMahon, Henry 87, 96, 97, 101
McMahon-Hussein Correspondence 67, 96, 97, 101
Mendes, Philip 202
Mitterrand, Alexandre 93
Montagu, Edwin 196
Montagu, Samuel 59
Morris, Benny 186
Moses (Prophet) 20, 25, 58, 102, 108
Mount Moriah 20
Moynihan, Patrick 208
MS St Louis 141
Munich Olympics massacre 188
Musa Kazim Pasha 112
Muslim Brotherhood 159
Napoleon 29, 130
Nasser, Gamal Abdel 203
Nazis or Nazi Germany 39, 126, 127, 128, 138, 139, 144, 145, 149, 151, 153, 154, 155, 163, 179, 207, 210, 211, 213
Nebi Musa riot 108, 109, 164
Netanyahu, Benjamin 84
Netanyahu, Benzion 84
Neturei Karta 200
Neue Freie Presse newspaper 48
Nitti, Francesco 93
Nosovitsky, Devorah 183

Nuremburg Laws 124
Odessa pogrom 62, 63, 125
Operation Wrath of God 190
Organization of Ukrainian Nationalists (OUP) 145
Orwell, George 38
Ottoman Empire 85, 87, 89, 91, 95, 96, 97, 104
Oz, Amos 179
Palace of Versailles 89
Palestine People's Party 160
Paris Conference 90, 105, 162
Passover feast massacre 188
Patterson, John Henry 83, 84
Peel Commission (1937) 116, 117, 118, 120, 121, 123
Peel Partition Plan 121
Persia 23, 24, 25, 52
Petyluria, Symon 129
Pharaoh Merenptah 18, 182
Philistines 28
Pinsker, Leon 41, 43, 48, 69, 126, 138, 197
Poland (treatment of Jews in) 34, 39, 94, 124, 131, 136, 139, 140, 143, 149, 201
Polish Peasants Party 140
Pompey 26
Portugal (massacre of Jews in) 32
Poznanski, Gustavus 196
Pronicheva, Dina 134
Reinharz, Jehuda 74
Rishon LeZion 43
Roman Empire 25, 28, 129
Rome (see also "Roman Empire") 25, 26, 32, 47
Roosevelt, Franklin D. 86, 140, 159
Rosh Pinna 43

Rothschild (2nd Baron Rothschild), Lord Lionel Walter 74, 79
Rothschild (Fourth Lord Rothschild), Jacob 81, 81, 94
Rothschild (Lord Rothschild), Nathaniel Mayer 58, 59
Rothschild Banking dynasty 55
Russia (treatment of Jews in) 34, 37, 38, 39, 48, 49, 56, 58, 59, 61, 66, 68, 133, 147, 196, 197, 201
Russian Revolution 53
Russo-Japanese War 63
Sacher, Harry 76
Samuel (Prophet) 19
Samuel, Herbert 75, 98, 108
San Remo Conference 92
Sand, Shlomo 200
Sandherr, Colonel 46
Saudi Arabia 97, 148
Scott, Charles Prestwich (C.P.) 76
Second Temple 26, 28, 110
Second World War 175
Second Zionist Congress 70, 84
Secret Protocols of the Elders of Zion 129, 205
Segev, Tom 147
Selecuid Dynasty 24
Shaw Commission Report 114
Sharett, Moshe 175
Silver, Abba Hillel 171
Simon Bar Kokhba 27, 82
Slonim, Shlomo 111
Sobibor concentration camp 136
Solomon 20, 21
Solomon's Temple 20, 21, 22, 23, 26, 29, 110
Soviet Union (see Russia)
Spain (treatment of Jews in) 32, 33, 125
SS Exodus 141, 164
Stadtcasino Basel 71
Start-Up Nation – the Story of Israel's Economic (Book by Dan Senor and Saul Singer) 191
Stern Gang (see also "Lehi") 164
Stern, Avraham 164
Suez Campaign 203
Suez Canal 203
Sultan of Turkey 55
Syria-Palaestina 26
Syria 24, 26, 96, 107, 118, 146, 176, 183, 187, 188, 198
Tel Aviv 67, 69, 106, 187, 181, 184, 188, 190, 237
The American Hebrew magazine 61
The City of Slaughter (poem by Hayim Nahman Bialik) 63, 64
The Jewish State (book by Theodor Herzl) 13, 49, 50
The New York Times 61
Theresiendstadt concentration camp 149
Third Zionist Congress 52
Tiberius 30
Times of London 87, 128
Tisha B'Av 22, 29
Titus 26, 28
Torah (see also "Five Books of Moses") 25
Transjordan 101, 115, 117, 164
Transjordan Memorandum 100, 102
Treaty of Lausanne 97
Treaty of Peace between Egypt and Israel 180
Treaty of Sevres 97
Treaty of Versailles 89
Treblinka concentration camp 136

INDEX

Truman, Harry S. 160, 165, 168, 183

Trumpeldor, Joseph 83, 84, 101

Tsfat 30, 110, 111

Twain, Mark 100

Twelve Tribes of Israel 18, 20

Twentieth Zionist Congress 117

Ukraine (treatment of Jews in) 36, 39, 134

United Nations General Assembly Resolution 181 (II): 172, 174, 181, 182

United Nations General Assembly Resolution 3379: 207, 209, 210

United Nations Security Council Resolution 242: 189

Ussishkin, Menachem 92

Wiesel, Elie 156

www.ingramcontent.com/pod-product-compliance
Lightning Source LLC
Chambersburg PA
CBHW070344240426
43671CB00013BA/2397